Sundown

To

Sunday

Contact the author
email: joao@machado-family.com

THANK YOU!

I would like to give special thanks to our Lord Jesus for laying the desire to write this book upon my heart. I do not know why but Jesus, I trust in you!

I would also like to thank my wonderful wife Darlene for never discouraging me while I pursued this rather odd endeavor, you are a true blessing from our Lord and I love you very much.

Lastly, a special thank you to my brother Paulino for doing the book cover art, thank you so much!

Table of Contents

TITLE	1
THANK YOU!	2
INTRODUCTION	4
THE SABBATH	8
GENESIS	12
KILL AND EAT	19
"I AM", The Covenant	31
THE EIGHTH DAY	55
JOHN PAUL II	59
APOSTOLIC LETTER	65
DIES DOMINI	75
DIES CHRISTI	90
DIES ECCLESIAE	104
DIES HOMINIS	135
DIES DIERUM	155
REFERENCE	171

INTRODUCTION

An unlikely book this is, to be written by someone who never considered himself much of an academic. After all, my formal education is in the Automotive and Diesel transportation industry but never the less, I feel compelled to put what I have learned in writing. The Sabbath is something that I have been studying for the last ten years. It really started when a good friend became a Seventh Day Adventist. One day, he and his wife, both of which I am still blessed to call good friends, asked me to go to a seminar at their church. The seminar was really about how if you worshiped or went to church on Sunday instead of Saturday (Sabbath) then you were basically going to Hell and if you belonged to the Catholic Church, well that is the Whore of Babylon and you really shouldn't be part of it. Even if you were not Catholic and still went to church on Sunday you were "paying homage" to the Whore of Babylon and that is not kosher. After that event, as we were walking to our cars, my good friend Eric even apologized. I don't believe he knew that it was going to be such a blatantly anti-Catholic discussion.

This, in your face approach, raised many questions in my mind, it tested me as a nominal Catholic and it challenged me in a way that I had never faced before. This eventually led me to buckle down and find the truth. I decided that I had to follow the Truth knowing full well that I may not like what I find.

Well, I found a lot and this book is written to give you a very high level overview, a meditation if you will, of how on one hand the Sabbath is still as relevant and intact as it was when Moses handed it to the Israelites and at the same time it is no longer binding to a baptized Christian.

I must warn you that there is probably nothing new in this book, there are no new insights or amazing revelations but only Scripture, the teachings of the Catholic Church on Scripture and a few of my own thoughts. I do not contend that this is a definitive authority on the subject of the Sabbath; after all, I have a Degree in Automotive and Diesel Technology not Theology.

The main reason I wrote this book is for the nominal Catholic. The average Catholic just does not understand the Sabbath and how it relates to their Christian Faith. Trust me on this one, it comes from experience. A good understanding of the Sabbath will deepen and strengthen your relationship with our Lord Jesus Christ.

For non-Catholics this book can be a good reference point to understand the teaching of the

Catholic Church on the Sabbath and how it relates to the Christian life.

My portion of this book is the minority. I have included the Apostolic Letter from John Paul II titled Dies Domini, because in that pastoral letter he explains the fullness of the reasons why Sunday or the first day of the week is held in such a high place in the Church. My portion of this book deals more with the apologetics, in a meditative sort of way, of why Christians no longer need to keep the Sabbath, which leads nicely into how we should keep the Lord's Day.

After reading this book, I would recommend reading Pope Benedict's Apostolic Exhortation, Sacramentum Caritatis (The sacrament of charity). It can be read online completely free of charge at:

http://www.vatican.va/holy_father/benedict_xvi/apost_e
xhortations/documents/hf_ben-
xvi_exh_20070222_sacramentum-caritatis_en.html

THE SABBATH

The Sabbath or *Shabbat* in Hebrew, is the Jewish day of rest. It is the seventh day of the week. In the modern English it is called Saturday but to an observing Jew it is still the Sabbath.

The Sabbath is the most important day to a Jew. It is the sign that G_d gave Israel as part of the Covenant made on Mount Sinai. This Covenant is part of the Decalogue or Ten Commandments, that was given to Moses by G_d to be handed to Israel. The Commandments were written on two tablets of stone with one commandment being the Sabbath and the stern warning to keep the Sabbath holy and to remember it.

The Sabbath has it's origins rooted in the first chapter of Genesis, but it is not until Israel is delivered from Egypt that G_d commands the day be observed. We first see the preparation of this when Israel was still a slave of Egypt. Moses gave the Israelites one day in seven to rest, a prefigurement of what was to come. Between this event and the Genesis account, there is no mention of the keeping of the Sabbath, obviously because the commandment to keep it had not yet been given.

The Pentateuch or the five books of Moses (the Torah), which includes Genesis, Exodus, Leviticus, Numbers and Deuteronomy along with New Testament will be our main focus in regards to the Sabbath and how it relates to the Christian life. Please don't get me wrong, the other Books of Scripture are still relevant but it is my opinion that they are in a supporting role and once you finish this book hopefully you will come to the same conclusion and see them in that way as well.

There is so much that can be discussed about the Sabbath. The various Jewish traditions from all over the world, how the Jewish people prepare for the Sabbath how they keep the Sabbath, what to do and what not to do. This would take a separate book in and of itself to explore. There are many Jewish books already out there that can give you all of these insights. What we will be meditating in this book is the main or fundamental reason for the Sabbath, why it was given, what it means and why it is important.

If you have not read the Bible, stop and put this book down and read at the very least the first five Books and the New Testament before you go any further. A basic understanding of Scripture is needed here. You cannot operate a car without reading the owners manual, well you can but it makes for a much larger learning curve. If I may quote St. Jerome, the great Saint and Scripture Scholar that translated the

Bible into Latin in the 5th Century, *"ignorance of Scripture is ignorance of Christ,"* so take the time to read the Bible first.

GENESIS

The Sabbath is rooted in the first account of Genesis, even if it is not called by name it is alluded to without question. It is a "type", a foreshadowing of the Sabbath that the Israelites would eventually have to uphold. Understanding the book of Genesis will shape our understanding of the Sabbath, especially when entering into the New Covenant that our Lord Jesus established.

The Book of Genesis can be broken down into three parts; the creation, the fall of man and the start of salvation history. We will focus on the creation accounts for it is here that we can truly learn the understanding of the Sabbath and our Lord Christ Jesus.

The story of creation is further broken into two parts, the first is Genesis 1. It is very methodical and systematic in how each day starts and ends, "*and there was evening and there was morning*". Each day starts with the evening and ends on the following evening, sundown to sundown. For each day something new is created, lights, oceans, land, sun, plants, animals and the last is man on the sixth day. On the seventh day, G_d finished His work and rested. This is an important note to take, that on the seventh day it was finished.

The second part of creation is Genesis 2, it shows us the relationship between G_d and man. G_d provided for man in every way, with food, shelter and when a suitable companion was not found for him, G_d created from him the perfect companion and called her woman.

"And Adam said: This now is bone of my bones, and flesh of my flesh; she shall be called woman, because she was taken out of man." Genesis2: 23(DRB)

The first account of Genesis is not meant to be a detailed historical or chronological account of the creation of the earth. Although it has elements of that, it is not its primary intent. Consider this. Which day was the sun created? In Genesis 1 we read the following;

"In the beginning G_d created heaven and earth. And the earth was void and empty, and darkness was upon the face of the deep; and the spirit of G_d moved over the waters. And G_d said: Be light made. And light was made.

And G_d saw the light that it was good; and he divided the light from the darkness. And he called the light Day and the darkness Night; and there was evening and morning one day."
GEN: 1-5 (DRB)

Then on the fourth day G_d says the following;

"And G_d said: Let there be lights made in the firmament of heaven, to divide the day and the night, and let them be for signs, and for seasons, and for days and years to shine in the firmament of heaven, and to give light upon the earth. And it was so done. And G_d made two great lights: a greater light to rule the day; and a lesser light to rule the night: and the stars. And he set them in the firmament of heaven to

shine upon the earth. And to rule the day and the night, and to divide the light and the darkness. And G_d saw that it was good. And the evening and morning were the fourth day."
GEN:14-19 (DRB)

So which day did G_d create light on, the first or third day? If you take a literalistic point of view, in which you believe each day is an actual 24hrs how do you reconcile which day the sun was created, for we know that there is only one sun? If on the other hand you say that one of those days was only figuratively speaking, then it is no longer a literalistic interpretation.

I am not saying that G_d did not make the Heavens and the Earth and everything in between, I wholeheartedly believe that G_d is the creator, no doubt in my mind. But it is not the intent of Genesis 1 to indicate that the Earth was created in a physical seven days, 24hr per day period. Consider for a moment that in Genesis 2:18, man has no helper so G_d brings forth all of the animals from the ground for him to name. In Genesis 1, man was created last, all of the animals were already created, which is correct? Even within Genesis 2:4, it says;

"These are the generations of the heaven and the earth, when they were created, in the day that the Lord G_d made the heaven and the earth: GEN:2-4(DRB)"

A day is neither a generation nor 6 days a generation, yet after the creation story that used the six days as the time frame of creation, Scripture seems to seemingly contradict itself or does it?

Genesis 1 is intended to show the order of importance of creation, with man being G_d's final creation and resting from His work on the seventh day. But the question as to why G_d rests or would even need to rest is a question that many ask. I have come to believe that it is for a very simple and direct reason. To convey to us that once He created man in His own image, there is nothing more to create! What more is there to create when man is created in the image and likeness of perfection, the creator Himself?

KILL AND EAT

Ooh, what kind of title is this? Well, I am referring to a vision Peter had when he was praying on the roof of the house of Simon, the tanner, in Joppa. You may be asking yourself what does food have to do with the Sabbath and it is a very good question indeed. I ask for your indulgence as I lay the groundwork for a point I will make later in the book.

The dietary restrictions put on the Israelites have often confused many, lay and scholars alike. It is a bit of a roller coaster ride when you look at what G_d says about what you should and should not eat throughout history. First, vegetables only before the great flood. Then after the flood everything could be eaten, then at Mount Sinai only certain fowl, meat, fish, vegetables but no blood or unleavened bread. Then in the New

Testament everything again. Confusing? You bet but not without reason.

Many think the dietary restrictions were for "health" reasons but this is just not the case. Actually let me rephrase that, not for physical health reasons. What I aim to show in this chapter is how food is tied to our salvation and how it relates to the Christian life. If the dietary restrictions were for the sole purpose of physical health, why would G_d give that restriction to Israel only? Why were the gentiles not bound to this dietary restriction as well?

In the book of Genesis, Noah is required to gather animals in groups of seven that are clean and groups of two that are not. Logic dictates a question here. If man ate nothing but vegetables before the great flood, why did Noah have to distinguish between clean and unclean? But what does "clean" and "unclean" mean anyway? Well, the term "clean" and "unclean" actually refers to "holy" and "unholy".

> *"And that you may have knowledge to discern between holy and unholy, between unclean and clean" LEV: 10 (DRB)*

In other words, a physical representation of a spiritual truth. You see, the animals themselves are not unclean, it is their actions. If you look at all of the dietary restrictions in Leviticus, look closely at the actions of the animals that are deemed clean and the ones deemed unclean. You will find that the difference between the two is their actions. Allow me to give an example. In the book of Isaiah, in the first chapter we read the following;

> *Hear, O ye heavens, and give ear, O earth, for the Lord hath spoken. I have brought up children, and exalted them: but they have despised me. The ox knoweth his owner and*

> *the ass his master's crib: but Israel hath not known me, and my people hath not understood.   Isaiah:1-2(DRB)*

Now, an ox is a clean animal and the action Isaiah attributes to that animal is, "it knows it's owner", and an ass (also a clean animal) knows it's master's manger. So by the same logic, an unclean animal would not know its owner, would not know its master.

In the Epistle of Barnabas, although not canonical and there is question as to whether he actually wrote the letter, the content points to this understanding of what clean and unclean mean. This Barnabas is Paul's companion from the book of Acts, here is chapter 10 from the Epistle of Barnabas;

> *Now, wherefore did Moses say, "You shall not eat the swine, nor the eagle, nor the hawk, nor the raven, nor any fish which is*

not possessed of scales?" He embraced three doctrines in his mind [in doing so]. Moreover, the Lord says to them in Deuteronomy, "And I will establish my ordinances among this people." Deuteronomy 4:1 Is there then not a command of G_d they should not eat [these things]? There is, but Moses spoke with a spiritual reference. For this reason he named the swine, as much as to say, "You shall not join yourself to men who resemble swine." For when they live in pleasure, they forget their Lord; but when they come to want, they acknowledge the Lord. And [in like manner] the swine, when it has eaten, does not recognize its master; but when hungry it cries out, and on receiving food is quiet again. "Neither shall you eat," says he "the eagle, nor the hawk, nor the kite, nor the raven." "You shall not join yourself," he means, "to such men as know not how to procure food for themselves by labour and sweat, but seize on that of others in their iniquity, and although wearing an aspect of simplicity, are on the watch to plunder others." So these birds, while they sit idle, inquire how they may devour the flesh of others, proving themselves pests [to all] by their wickedness. "And you shall not eat," he says, "the lamprey, or the polypus, or the cuttlefish." He means, "You shall not join yourself or be like to such men as are ungodly to the end, and are condemned to death." In like manner as those fishes, above accursed, float in the deep, not swimming [on the surface] like the rest, but make their abode in the mud which lies at the bottom. Moreover, "You shall not," he says, "eat the hare." Wherefore? "You shall not be a corrupter of boys, nor like such." Because the hare multiplies, year by year, the places of its conception; for as many years as it lives so many it has. Moreover, "You shall not eat the hyena." He means, "You shall not be an adulterer, nor a corrupter, nor be like to them that are such." Wherefore? Because that animal annually changes its sex, and is at one time male, and at another female. Moreover, he has rightly detested the weasel. For he means, "You shall not be like to those whom we hear of as committing wickedness with the mouth, on account of their uncleanness; nor shall you be joined to those impure women who commit iniquity with the mouth. For this animal conceives by the mouth." Moses then issued three doctrines concerning meats with a spiritual significance; but they received them according to fleshly desire, as if he had merely spoken of [literal] meats. David, however, comprehends the knowledge of the three doctrines, and speaks in like manner: "Blessed is the man who has not walked in the counsel of the ungodly," even as the fishes [referred to] go in darkness to the depths [of the sea]; "and has not stood in the way of sinners," even as those who profess to fear the Lord, but go astray like swine; "and has not sat in the seat of scorners," even as those birds that lie in wait for prey. Take a full and firm grasp of this spiritual knowledge. But Moses says still further, "You shall eat every animal that is cloven-footed and ruminant." What does he mean? [The ruminant animal denotes him] who, on receiving food, recognizes Him that nourishes him, and being satisfied by Him, is visibly made glad. Well spoke [Moses], having respect to the commandment. What, then, does he *mean? That we ought to join ourselves to those that fear the Lord, those who meditate in their heart on the commandment which they have received, those who both utter the judgments of the Lord and observe them, those who know that meditation is a work of gladness, and who ruminate upon the word of the Lord. But what means the cloven-footed? That the righteous man also walks in this world, yet looks forward to the holy state [to come]. Behold how well Moses legislated. But how was it possible for them to understand or comprehend these things? We then, rightly understanding his commandments, explain them as the Lord intended. For this purpose He circumcised our ears and our hearts, that we might understand these things. (<u>newadvent.org</u>)*

Now an Israelite can become unclean if they touched a dead clean animal that died on its own or was killed by a wild beast. That person would be considered "unclean" but only until that evening and after they bathed and washed their clothes. (Lev17:14) So how can a person be "unclean" just by touching an animal and not eating of it?

To be "clean" is to be in under the law, to be free of sin, to be obedient to the Covenant that the G_d of Abraham made with them. It is to be set apart from the Gentiles, it is to be Holy!

Peter the Apostle had a vision while he was praying on the roof of the house of Simon, the tanner. The vision instructed him to kill and eat animals that were not clean and Peter responded that he had never eaten anything unclean, then the Angel instructed him that;

"what G_d has made clean he should not call unclean." (Acts 10).

Did Christ die for the salvation of animals or man? Man of course, but the vision has a two fold meaning as Peter soon found out when he went to the house of

Cornelius. Peter soon realized that salvation had come to the Gentiles and this posed an obvious question. The Gentiles ate unclean foods so what should be done in regards to the diet of the Gentiles? The Counsel of Jerusalem was convened and after listening to the testimony of Peter about what had happened in Joppa, it was determined that the newly converted Gentiles had to only abstain from food polluted by idols, unlawful marriage, meat from strangled animals and from blood. (Acts15, 19-20) It also signifies that the dietary law was no longer binding to Jew or a Gentile for that matter.

St. Paul further emphasizes this in his different letters:

> *Now him that is weak in faith, take unto you: not in disputes about thoughts. For one believeth that he may eat all things: but he that is weak, let him eat herbs. Let not him that eateth, despise him that eateth not: and he that eateth not, let him not judge him that eateth. For G_d hath taken him to him. Who art thou that judgest another*

man's servant? To his own lord he standeth or falleth. And he shall stand: for G_d is able to make him stand. For one judgeth between day and day: and another judgeth every day: let every man abound in his own sense. He that regardeth the day, regardeth it unto the Lord. And he that eateth, eateth to the Lord: for he giveth thanks to G_d. And he that eateth not, to the Lord he eateth not, and giveth thanks to G_d. For none of us liveth to himself; and no man dieth to himself. For whether we live, we live unto the Lord; or whether we die, we die unto the Lord. Therefore, whether we live, or whether we die, we are the Lord's. ROM:14,1-8(DRB)

Let no man therefore judge you in meat or in drink, or in respect of a festival day, or of the new moon, or of the sabbaths, which are a shadow of things to come, but the body is of Christ. COL: 2,16-17(DRB)

St. Paul, a self proclaimed "zealot for the law" (ACTS:

22,3) taught in all of the Jewish Laws now sees no reason for converts to keep the dietary law, in fact he calls those who still hold to keeping the dietary law "weak in faith"!

"I AM", The Covenant

Turning to the twelve He asks, *"but who do you say that I am"*, Simon Peter spoke up and said; *"you are the Christ"!*

Do you understand the ramifications attached to this conversation? If you answer this question just as if Jesus was standing in front of you, would you respond in the same way Peter did? There are only two possible answers to this question, either Jesus is who He says He is or not. There is no in between, no sitting on the fence, no gray area. One must either believe Him or not.

Reading the Gospels, it is very evident if not completely apparent that everything Jesus did and said was to make us believe that He is the Son of G_d. All of the miracles He performed were for this purpose, to convince us that He was sent from G_d!

I cannot of myself do anything. As I hear, so I judge. And my judgment is just because I seek not my own will but the will of him that sent me. If I bear witness of myself, my witness is not true. There is another that beareth witness of me: and I know that the witness which he witnesseth of me is true. You sent to John: and he gave testimony to the truth. But I receive not testimony from man: but I say these things, that you may be saved. He was a burning and a shining light: and you were willing for a time to rejoice in his light. But I have a greater testimony than that of John: for the works which the Father hath given me to perfect, the works themselves which I do, give testimony of me, that the Father hath sent me. And the Father himself who hath sent me hath given testimony of me. JHN: 5,30-37(DRB)

When Jesus speaks to His disciples and explains

that He is the bread from Heaven, that they (the disciples) are to eat His flesh, to drink His blood, many of them found this hard to endure and many disciples turned back to their former way of life and no longer followed Him. (John6:66) Jesus then turning to the twelve asks if they too will also walk away. Simon Peter answered Him, *"Lord, to whom shall we go? Thou hast the words of eternal life"*. JOHN 6:69(DRB) You see, the twelve had come to believe that Jesus is the Son of G_d and that makes him equal to G_d, which makes Him G_d. The other disciples did not believe that He was the Son of G_d; they did not believe that He was sent by the Father even though He worked so many miracles for them. When it came to complete trust and abandonment, their faith was just not there.

The 6th Chapter of St. John's Gospel is very difficult for many to swallow, no pun intended. But you must remember that Jesus always spoke to His disciples in parables except on this occasion. When Jesus would teach in parables He always turned to His twelve chosen disciples and explained the parable to them afterward.

> *And his disciples asked him what this parable might be. To whom he said: To you it is given to know the mystery of the kingdom of G_d; ; but to the rest in parables, that seeing they may not see and hearing may not understand. LUK:8, 9-10(DRB)*

So by asking the twelve if they too would walk away Jesus in fact affirmed that He did not speak in a parable when He said that they must eat His flesh and drink His blood.

When Jesus stands before the Priests of Israel and says, "I AM", He is echoing back to when Moses was on Mount Sinai, when G_d tells Moses his name "I AM". That is to say, I am G_d, I commanded Moses to lead my people out of Egypt, I gave Moses the Commandments, before Abraham was, "I AM" (JHN8: 58).

When Jesus says, *"I and the Father are one" (JHN:10-30)*, He is reiterating what He had already told them once before;

> *"Hear, O Israel, the Lord our G_d is one Lord" (DEU: 6-6).*

When Jesus is asked why His disciples are plucking the ears of corn to eat on the Sabbath, Jesus says;

> *"And he said to them: The Sabbath was made for man, and not man for the Sabbath. Therefore the Son of man is Lord of the Sabbath also." MRK: 2-27 (DRB)*

That is to say, I made that Covenant with you on Mount Sinai; I am the one who gave it to you. The Covenant I made with you is for your salvation not the salvation of a day.

It is interesting to note, you will not find Jesus preaching the keeping of the Sabbath, and you will not find any of the Apostles preaching the keeping of the Sabbath in the Gospels. In fact, almost every time Sabbath is mentioned in the Gospels, it is usually someone claiming that Jesus is breaking the Sabbath or that His disciples are breaking the Sabbath.

After the Exodus, the deliverance from Egypt, G_d makes a Covenant with Israel, this is the Sabbath, the Jewish *Shabbat*. Now, this Covenant is with Israel and only Israel.

> *And the Lord spoke to Moses, saying: Speak to the children of Israel, and thou shalt say to them: See that thou keep my Sabbath: because*

it is a sign between me and you in your generations: that you may know that I am the Lord, who sanctify you. EXO: 31, 12-13(DRB)

Notice that this Covenant is between G_d and Israel's generations. This is very important because it shows that this Covenant will in fact be intact until the end of time, until Jesus' second coming. But how can this be if none of the Apostles even mention the keeping of the Sabbath, nor did Jesus for that matter?

If Jesus is indeed G_d, is it not He who gives the Sermon on the Mount, is it not the same person who also gave Moses the Commandments on Mount Sinai? By looking at both the Commandments that were given on Mount Sinai and the Sermon on the Mount, we see the Commandments explained. On Mount Sinai we are told (with the exception of the Sabbath and honoring your parents) what not to do, the Sermon on the Mount tell us what we aught to do. So why, did Jesus not preach the keeping of the Sabbath during the Sermon on the Mount? Did He expect the Sabbath commandment to be broken? No! He came to fulfill the Law.

> *Do not think that I am come to destroy the law, or the prophets. I am not come to destroy, but to fulfill. For amen I say unto you, till heaven and earth pass, not one jot, or one tittle shall not pass of the law, till all be fulfilled. MAT: 5, 17-18(DRB)*

So what does it mean to fulfill the law? Jesus was asked which of the Commandments was the greatest.

> *But the Pharisees hearing that he had silenced the Sadducees, came together And one of them, a doctor of the law, asking him, tempting him Master, which is the greatest commandment in the law? Jesus said to him: Thou shalt love the Lord thy G_d with thy whole heart, and with thy whole soul, and with thy whole mind. This is the greatest and the first commandment. And*

the second is like to this: Thou shalt love thy neighbor as thyself. On these two commandments dependeth the whole law and the prophets. MAT: 22, 34-40 (DRB)

This is to say, *these two commandments are the two tablets that I gave Moses!* The Ten Commandments can be divided into two parts, this first half and the second half. The first half, the first tablet is like the first great commandment, to love G_d with all your heart mind and soul. The second half, the second tablet is like the second great commandment, to love your neighbor as yourself.

Do you remember the story of the rich young man? Jesus was asked a very interesting question in the Gospel of Matthew;

And behold one came and said to him: Good master, what good shall I do that I may have life everlasting? Who said to him: Why asketh thou me concerning good? One is good, G_d. But if thou wilt enter into life, keep the commandments. He said to him: Which? And Jesus said: Thou shalt do no murder, Thou shalt not commit adultery, Thou shalt not steal, Thou shalt not bear false witness. Honour thy father and thy mother: and, Thou shalt love thy neighbor as thyself. The young man saith to him: All these I have kept from my youth, what is yet wanting to me? Jesus saith to him: If thou wilt be perfect, go sell what thou hast, and give to the poor, and thou shalt have treasure in heaven: and come follow me. And when the young man had heard this word, he went away sad: for he had great possessions. MAT: 19, 16-22(DRB)

The first thing I noticed in this story is that the young man appears to be very prideful. He had "kept all of the Commandments" but Scripture clearly tells us that no man could keep them perfectly. When Jesus runs through the Commandments, the Sabbath is seemingly missing, Jesus makes no mention of it. He runs through a litany of the commandments except the Sabbath.

Now when Jesus enters Jerusalem on Palm Sunday on an ass, the start of the Jewish Passover is at hand. Jesus will become the new Passover lamb, all of the events that proceed for the next eight days echo directly back to the book of Exodus. The events of Israel's Passover are but a shadow of the true Lamb that will be sacrificed so that sins may be forgiven. Again, if you do not know the story of the Passover and you have not read the first five books of the Bible, stop right here and go and read them. I will assume that you have read them from this point on. The reason I am stressing the importance of reading those books, especially Genesis, is because the events of that fateful Passover with Jesus not only echoes back to Israel's deliverance from Egypt but it also echoes directly back to the creation story itself.

Jesus is called by Paul the "New Adam" (ROM5:14) and for good reason. Just as the Passover was a shadow of the Last Supper, the foundation of the Crucifixion was laid down in the story of creation in the book of Genesis. The two events merge at this point in time. Consider for a moment some of the miracles that Jesus performed and how they resemble the events in Genesis, like the walking on water towards the disciples on the boat. In Genesis, *and the spirit of G_d moved over the waters*. The catching of the fish by Peter where the nets were completely full. In Genesis, *and G_d created the great whales, and every living and moving creature, which the waters brought forth, according to their kinds, and every winged fowl according to its kind*. The withering of the fig tree because it did not bear fruit. In Genesis, *and the earth brought forth the green herb, and such as yieldeth seed according to its kind, and the tree that beareth fruit, having seed each one according to its kind.* The storm with Jesus sleeping on a cushion and He calms the waters and the wind. In Genesis, *and G_d called the dry land, Earth; and the gathering together of the waters, he called Seas.* And the Apostles said to one another *"Who is this that the wind and seas obey Him?" MRK: 4, 40(DRB)*

This is why St. John calls Jesus the author of life (ACTS3:15), for He created everything and He has power and dominion over it.

Allow me to tell you a little story before we go on. I used to help out at the RCIA class at my old Parish in Lodi, CA . The Deacon told us a story of how the previous year, the RCIA class had been studying the Trinity. The Deacon decided to ask the Rector of the Parish to come and give a talk on the Trinity. The Father was an old Irish priest, very mild mannered and the Deacon had told him that the students were well versed on the theology of the Trinity and were anxiously waiting for the talk by the Father. So the evening came and he addressed the class and looking around at everyone he says the following; "The Trinity is a mystery, good night". A humbling reminder that we can only understand so much with our finite minds, some things are just a mystery and we must keep that in mind at all times.

The Last Supper is the affirmation of what Jesus had told His disciples about Him being the Bread that has come down from Heaven and that they must eat His flesh and drink His blood. That is the reason for the dietary prohibition of eating unleavened bread and the drinking of blood. For He is the bread that will rise, His blood is the blood that will give life! *For the life of all flesh is in the blood. LEV17: 14(DRB)*

John's Gospel, chapter 6:

Amen, amen I say unto you: He that believeth in me, hath everlasting life. I am the bread of life. Your fathers did eat manna in the desert, and are dead. This is the bread which cometh down from heaven; that if any man eat of it, he may not die. I am the living bread which came down from heaven. If any man eats of this bread, he shall live for ever; and the bread that I will give, is my flesh, for the life of the world. The Jews therefore strove among themselves, saying: How can this man give us his flesh to eat? Then Jesus said to them: Amen, amen I say unto you: Except you eat the flesh of the Son of man, and drink his blood, you shall not have life in you. He that eateth my flesh, and drinketh my blood, hath everlasting life: and I will raise him up in the last day. For my flesh is meat indeed: and my blood is drink indeed. He that eateth my flesh, and drinketh my blood, abideth in me, and I in him. As the living Father hath sent me, and I live by the Father; so he that eateth me, the same also shall live by me. This is the bread that came down from heaven. Not as your fathers did eat manna, and are dead. He that eateth this bread shall live for ever. (JHN: 6, 47-59)

This is why when Saul met Jesus on the road to Damascus, Jesus tells him, *"Saul, Saul why do you persecute me?"* Notice Jesus does not say, persecute my Church or my followers, He says "me". This is because the members of His Church are united to Him, they abide in Him and He abides in them. It is in this great mystery called the Eucharist that this takes place. This is the New Covenant, the new and everlasting covenant. HEB13: 20(DRB)

Do you remember in the book of Numbers when the man was caught picking up sticks on the Sabbath? G_d struck him down dead! That was to show us that to break the Covenant means death, Jesus here tells us that by keeping His New Covenant it means life.

When the Virgin Mary laid the baby Jesus in the manger, a feeding trough, it was a shadow of what was to come, what His whole mission was. There in the manger, was the bread of life surrounded by all of the clean animals that feed from the manger.

All living things on Earth survive on the eating of what has died, even vegetarians must admit this as well for it is a self evident fact that life depends on death to survive. No matter if it is an animal, fish or vegetable.

So too if we want eternal life we must eat of that which is eternal.

It is the spirit that quickeneth: the flesh profiteth nothing. The words that I have spoken to you are spirit and life. (John6: 64)

When Israel started complaining about their journey in the desert, G_d sent serpents to afflict them because of their sins and many died. When Moses prayed for Israel, G_d commanded Moses to fashion a bronze serpent and put it on a pole and instructed Moses to tell the people if bitten to look upon it and they would be healed. St. Francis De Sales made an excellent observation in one of his sermons for Lent. The bronze serpent on its own has no power to heal the people it is their faith and obedience that heals them , for if they did not look upon the serpent they would not live. The same can also be said for the Passover. If the Children of Israel did not do everything that G_d had instructed them, by putting the lamb's blood on the door lentils and to actually eat of the Passover lamb the first born in that family would have perished. In other words, it is not enough to believe, you must obey and do what He tells you. But for Jesus, this has a two-fold meaning, for Jesus is both man and G_d. Him being lifted up on the cross we believe, and by obeying His commandment to *"do this in memory of me"*; we obtain what He promised, eternal life...this is the Eucharist.

But how can the bread and wine become the body and blood of Jesus? This is a question of faith.

When Jesus cured the leper on the road how did He do it? He commanded it! When He brought Lazarus back from the dead, how did He do it? He commanded it! When Jesus calmed the wind and the seas, how did He do it? He commanded it! When Jesus turned the water into wine, how did He do it? He commanded it! Every miracle that Jesus performed was by His very word. So when Jesus, after giving thanks to the Father, takes the bread, breaks the bread and blesses it, lifts it up and says, "This is my body"! What did that bread just become? That bread, like every other element in the universe had no choice but to obey its creator! This is a great mystery; the creator is holding Himself, sacrificing Himself, giving Himself for His creation.

In the Bible, every time a person ripped or tore their clothes it was in shear pain or agony. When Jacob received word that Joseph's clothes had been found and torn, Jacob concluded that wild beasts had eaten Joseph and he tore his garments because of the sheer loss and hurt over his son. We see G_d the Father doing the same thing, for when Jesus gave up His spirit the veil in the Holy of Holies torn in two. If you do not know what the Holy of Holies is or the veil that separates the Holy of Holies, read up on it!

The Eucharist is the New Covenant. This New Covenant starts where the Sabbath stops. The Sabbath becomes fulfilled upon the death of Jesus on the cross. Remember, the Sabbath Covenant was made between G_d and Israel, so the only way that either one can be released from the Covenant is for one of them to die. When Jesus says He has come to fulfill the law, He is referring to His death. By His death, the Sabbath Covenant is released and there by fulfilled. A Covenant is like a marriage and Peter understood this and conveyed it in his letter to the Hebrews;

And therefore he is the mediator of the New

Testament: that by means of his death, for the redemption of those transgressions, which were under the former testament, they that are called may receive the promise of eternal inheritance. For where there is a testament, the death of the testator must of necessity come in. For a testament is of force, after men are dead: otherwise it is as yet of no strength, whilst the testator liveth. HEB: 9, 15-17(DRB)

This is why the Angel told Peter during his vision in Joppa that "what G_d has made clean to not call unclean" The Angel was referring to the Law no longer binding because G_d had fulfilled the Law through the death of Jesus the Christ. Like a marriage, when one spouse dies, the other is freed from the covenant of marriage. (ROM7: 2, 1COR 7:39)

Now, as for the Jew, the New Covenant is not bound on them until they come to see Christ as G_d. This is why after Paul meets Jesus on the road to Damascus, he no longer observed the dietary Law or the Sabbath, for he understood the difference. This is also why St. Paul says there is a "veil over their eyes", referring to the Jews. This veil, G_d has left in tact on purpose to fulfill His purpose and will be there until the end of time. As long as this veil is in place they cannot see Jesus as G_d and therefore cannot see that the Law including the Sabbath has been fulfilled. If a Jew is to come to Christ, they are released from the Law by way of Baptism;

> *Know you not that all we, who are baptized in Christ Jesus, are baptized in his death? ROM: 6-3 (DRB)*

The two Covenants, the Sabbath and the Eucharist, these are the wine skins Jesus refers to when He says:

> *People do not put new wine into old wineskins. Otherwise the skins burst, the wine spills out, and the skins are ruined. Rather, they pour new*

wine into fresh wineskins, and both are preserved." MAT: 9-17(DRB)

This is also why the New and Everlasting Covenant will not fade away, for Jesus who made this Covenant at the Last Supper will never die again, for He is risen, truly risen to the Father and is seated at the right hand of the Father. This New Covenant He makes between himself and His Bride the Church. For just like Adam was put into a deep sleep and woman came from the side of Adam, Jesus hanging on the cross is pierced on His side and out comes blood and water, the two elements of life one carnal one spiritual, the Church, His Bride! But before His death on the cross He makes it perfectly known who He is when on that Good Friday afternoon, when the day is passing from the sixth day to the seventh, he echoes back to Genesis and utters as His last words, *it is finished.*

THE EIGHTH DAY

This chapter is but a short introduction into John Paul II, Apostolic letter, for in that he lays out the teaching of the Church on The Day of The Lord. As we discussed in the previous chapter, the Eucharist is the new Sabbath, the New Covenant. It stands to reason that this Eucharist must take place on a day but which day?

The order of the seven day week is first and foremost the reminder of where we come from, whom we come from and to whom we hopefully shall return. The cycle of the seven days is unbroken from the time the Sabbath was given to until today. Before the Law was given at Mount Sinai, Scripture has no definitive form of the week with the Sabbath. The months were there and the number of days were there but the

Sabbath is not found until it was given to Israel in the book of Exodus. One of the first clear signs we see, outside of Genesis, was while Israel was still a slave under Egypt. When Moses, while still under the rule of the Pharaoh, gave the Israelites one day in seven to rest, a shadow of what was to come.

But the first day of the week, or the eighth day as it is also known, is riddled with typology in the Old Testament. When you read Genesis, Chapters 7 and 8, you will find that Noah's ark came to rest on the seventh month after Noah's 100th year, after eight months the water began to withdraw and the tops of the mountains could be seen. Then on the first day of the first month of Noah's six hundred and first year, Noah opened the covering to the ark and they exited the ark, eight in all.

For if G_d spared not the angels that sinned, but delivered them, drawn down by infernal ropes to the lower hell, unto torments, to be reserved unto judgment. And spared not the original world, but preserved Noe, the eighth person, the preacher of justice, bringing in the flood upon the world of the unG_dly. 2Peter: 2-5(DRB)

This is a constant and recurring theme throughout Scripture, with the first day and the eighth day having high significance. For a week has only seven days, when the eighth day is mentioned, it is always in reference to the return to the first day of the week following the Sabbath, the completion of a cycle.

Now the celebration of the Eucharist is not isolated to just one day of the week for as it is foretold in the book of Malachi, the last book of the Old Testament. The prophet Malachi foretells of how a clean offering by the Gentiles would be offered from sunrise to sunset.

For from the rising of the sun even to the going down, my name is great among the Gentiles, and in every place there is sacrifice, and there is offered to my name a clean oblation: for my name is great among the Gentiles, saith the Lord of hosts. MAL:1-11(DRB)

Now there is only one sacrifice that is acceptable to G_d and that is the Lamb of G_d, Jesus! In the Eucharist this prophecy is fulfilled. The Eucharist is offered everyday but it is on Sunday, the first day of the week that this reality is brought to the pinnacle, the summit of our Faith.

Jesus tells us that He is the light of the world, in the book of Revelation, the last book of the Bible, He tells us that He is the Alpha and the Omega, the beginning and the end, the first and the last and it is on the first day of the week in the book of Genesis that G_d says, *let there be light*!

JOHN PAUL II

Apostolic Letter

Dies Domini

INDEX – DIES DOMINI

Introduction

Chapter I
DIES DOMINI

The Celebration of the Creator's Work

"Through him all things were made" (*Jn* 1:3)

"In the beginning, G_d created the heavens and the earth" (*Gn* 1:1) "*Shabbat*": the Creator's joyful rest

"G_d blessed the seventh day and made it holy" (*Gn*2:3)

"To keep holy" by "remembering"

From the Sabbath to Sunday

Chapter II

DIES CHRISTI

The Day of the Risen Lord and of the Gift of the Holy Spirit.

The weekly Easter
The first day of the week
Growing distinction from the Sabbath
The day of the new creation
The eighth day: image of eternity
The day of Christ-Light
The day of the gift of the Spirit
The day of faith
An indispensable day!

Chapter III

DIES ECCLESIAE

The Eucharistic Assembly: Heart of Sunday
The presence of the Risen Lord
The Eucharistic assembly
The Sunday Eucharist
The day of the Church
A pilgrim people
The day of hope
The table of the word
The table of the Body of Christ
Easter banquet and fraternal gathering
From Mass to "mission"
The Sunday obligation
A joyful celebration in song
A celebration involving all
Other moments of the Christian Sunday
Sunday assemblies without a priest
Radio and television

Chapter IV

DIES HOMINIS

Sunday: Day of Joy, Rest and Solidarity
The "full joy" of Christ
The fulfillment of the Sabbath
The day of rest
A day of solidarity

Chapter V

DIES DIERUM

Sunday: the Primordial Feast, Revealing the Meaning of Time
Christ the Alpha and Omega of time
Sunday in the Liturgical Year
Conclusion

APOSTOLIC LETTER

DIES DOMINI

OF THE HOLY FATHER
JOHN PAUL II
TO THE BISHOPS, CLERGY AND FAITHFUL
OF THE CATHOLIC CHURCH
ON KEEPING THE LORD'S DAY HOLY

My esteemed Brothers in the Episcopate
and the Priesthood,
Dear Brothers and Sisters!

1. The Lord's Day — as Sunday was called from

Apostolic times(1) — has always been accorded special attention in the history of the Church because of its close connection with the very core of the Christian mystery. In fact, in the weekly reckoning of time Sunday recalls the day of Christ's Resurrection. It is *Easter* which returns week by week, celebrating Christ's victory over sin and death, the fulfilment in him of the first creation and the dawn of "the new creation" (cf. *2 Cor* 5:17). It is the day which recalls in grateful adoration the world's first day and looks forward in active hope to "the last day", when Christ will come in glory (cf. *Acts* 1:11; 1 *Th* 4:13-17) and all things will be made new (cf. *Rev* 21:5).

Rightly, then, the Psalmist's cry is applied to Sunday: "This is the day which the Lord has made: let us rejoice and be glad in it" (*Ps* 118:24). This invitation to joy, which the Easter liturgy makes its own, reflects the astonishment which came over the women who, having seen the crucifixion of Christ, found the tomb empty when they went there "very early on the first day after the Sabbath" (*Mk* 16:2). It is an invitation to relive in some way the experience of the two disciples of Emmaus, who felt their hearts "burn within them" as the Risen One walked with them on the road, explaining the Scriptures and revealing himself in "the breaking of the bread" (cf. *Lk* 24:32,35). And it echoes the joy — at first uncertain and then overwhelming — which the Apostles experienced on the evening of that same day, when they were visited by the Risen Jesus and received the gift of his peace and of his Spirit (cf. *Jn* 20:19-23).

2. The Resurrection of Jesus is the fundamental event upon which Christian faith rests (cf. *1 Cor* 15:14). It is an astonishing reality, fully grasped in the light of faith, yet historically attested to by those who were privileged to see the Risen Lord. It is a wondrous event which is not only absolutely unique in human history, but which lies *at the very heart of the mystery of time*. In fact, "all time belongs to [Christ] and all the ages", as the evocative liturgy of the Easter Vigil recalls in preparing the Paschal Candle. Therefore, in commemorating the day of Christ's Resurrection not just once a year but every Sunday, the Church seeks to indicate to every generation the true fulcrum of history, to which the mystery of the world's origin and its final destiny leads.

It is right, therefore, to claim, in the words of a fourth

century homily, that "the Lord's Day" is "the lord of days".(2) Those who have received the grace of faith in the Risen Lord cannot fail to grasp the significance of this day of the week with the same deep emotion which led Saint Jerome to say: "Sunday is the day of the Resurrection, it is the day of Christians, it is our day". (3) For Christians, Sunday is "the fundamental feastday",(4) established not only to mark the succession of time but to reveal time's deeper meaning.

3. The fundamental importance of Sunday has been recognized through two thousand years of history and was emphatically restated by the Second Vatican Council: "Every seven days, the Church celebrates the Easter mystery. This is a tradition going back to the Apostles, taking its origin from the actual day of Christ's Resurrection — a day thus appropriately designated 'the Lord's Day'."(5) Paul VI emphasized this importance once more when he approved the new General Roman Calendar and the Universal Norms which regulate the ordering of the Liturgical Year.(6) The coming of the Third Millennium, which calls believers to reflect upon the course of history in the light of Christ, also invites them to rediscover with new intensity the meaning of Sunday: its "mystery", its

celebration, its significance for Christian and human life.

I note with pleasure that in the years since the Council this important theme has prompted not only many interventions by you, dear Brother Bishops, as teachers of the faith, but also different pastoral strategies which — with the support of your clergy — you have developed either individually or jointly. On the threshold of the Great Jubilee of the Year 2000, it has been my wish to offer you this Apostolic Letter in order to support your pastoral efforts in this vital area. But at the same time I wish to turn to all of you, Christ's faithful, as though I were spiritually present in all the communities in which you gather with your Pastors each Sunday to celebrate the Eucharist and "the Lord's Day". Many of the insights and intuitions which prompt this Apostolic Letter have grown from my episcopal service in Krakow and, since the time when I assumed the ministry of Bishop of Rome and Successor of Peter, in the visits to the Roman parishes which I have made regularly on the Sundays of the different seasons of the Liturgical Year. I see this Letter as continuing the lively exchange which I am always happy to have with the faithful, as I reflect with you on the meaning of Sunday and underline the reasons for living Sunday as truly "the Lord's Day", also in the changing circumstances of our own times.

4. Until quite recently, it was easier in traditionally Christian countries to keep Sunday holy because it was an almost universal practice and because, even in the organization of civil society, Sunday rest was considered a fixed part of the work schedule. Today, however, even in those countries which give legal sanction to the festive character of Sunday, changes in socioeconomic conditions have often led to profound modifications of social behaviour and hence of the character of Sunday. The custom of the "weekend" has become more widespread, a weekly period of respite, spent perhaps far from home and often involving participation in cultural, political or sporting activities which are usually held on free days. This social and cultural phenomenon is by no means without its positive aspects if, while respecting true values, it can contribute to people's development and to the advancement of the life of society as a whole. All of this responds not only to the need for rest, but also to the need for celebration which is inherent in our humanity. Unfortunately, when Sunday loses its

fundamental meaning and becomes merely part of a "weekend", it can happen that people stay locked within a horizon so limited that they can no longer see "the heavens".(7) Hence, though ready to celebrate, they are really incapable of doing so.

The disciples of Christ, however, are asked to avoid any confusion between the celebration of Sunday, which should truly be a way of keeping the Lord's Day holy, and the "weekend", understood as a time of simple rest and relaxation. This will require a genuine spiritual maturity, which will enable Christians to "be what they are", in full accordance with the gift of faith, always ready to give an account of the hope which is in them (cf. 1 *Pt* 3:15). In this way, they will be led to a deeper understanding of Sunday, with the result that, even in difficult situations, they will be able to live it in complete docility to the Holy Spirit.

5. From this perspective, the situation appears somewhat mixed. On the one hand, there is the example of some young Churches, which show how fervently Sunday can be celebrated, whether in urban areas or in widely scattered villages. By contrast, in other parts of

the world, because of the sociological pressures already noted, and perhaps because the motivation of faith is weak, the percentage of those attending the Sunday liturgy is strikingly low. In the minds of many of the faithful, not only the sense of the centrality of the Eucharist but even the sense of the duty to give thanks to the Lord and to pray to him with others in the community of the Church, seems to be diminishing.

It is also true that both in mission countries and in countries evangelized long ago the lack of priests is such that the celebration of the Sunday Eucharist cannot always be guaranteed in every community.

6. Given this array of new situations and the questions which they prompt, it seems more necessary than ever *to recover the deep doctrinal foundations* underlying the Church's precept, so that the abiding value of Sunday in the Christian life will be clear to all the faithful. In doing this, we follow in the footsteps of the age-old tradition of the Church, powerfully restated by the Second Vatican Council in its teaching that on Sunday "Christian believers should come together, in order to commemorate the suffering, Resurrection and glory of

the Lord Jesus, by hearing G_d's Word and sharing the Eucharist, and to give thanks to G_d who has given them new birth to a living hope through the Resurrection of Jesus Christ from the dead (cf. *1 Pt 1:3*)".(8)

7. The duty to keep Sunday holy, especially by sharing in the Eucharist and by relaxing in a spirit of Christian joy and fraternity, is easily understood if we consider the many different aspects of this day upon which the present Letter will focus our attention.

Sunday is a day which is at the very heart of the Christian life. From the beginning of my Pontificate, I have not ceased to repeat: "Do not be afraid! Open, open wide the doors to Christ!".(9) In the same way, today I would strongly urge everyone to rediscover Sunday: *Do not be afraid to give your time to Christ!* Yes, let us open our time to Christ, that he may cast light upon it and give it direction. He is the One who knows the secret of time and the secret of eternity, and he gives us "his day" as an ever new gift of his love. The rediscovery of this day is a grace which we must implore, not only so that we may live the demands of faith to the full, but also so that we may respond concretely to the deepest human yearnings. Time given to Christ is never time lost, but is rather time gained, so that our relationships and indeed our whole life may become more profoundly human.

DIES DOMINI

CHAPTER I

The Celebration of the Creator's Work

"*Through him all things were made*" (*Jn* 1:3)

8. For the Christian, Sunday is above all an Easter celebration, wholly illumined by the glory of the Risen Christ. It is the festival of the "new creation". Yet, when understood in depth, this aspect is inseparable from what the first pages of Scripture tell us of the plan of G_d in the creation of the world. It is true that the Word was made flesh in "the fullness of time" (*Gal* 4:4); but it is also true that, in virtue of the mystery of his identity as the eternal Son of the Father, he is the origin and end of the universe. As John writes in the Prologue of his Gospel: "Through him all things were made, and without him was made nothing that was made" (1:3). Paul too stresses this in writing to the Colossians: "In

him all things were created, in heaven and on earth, visible and invisible .... All things were created through him and for him" (1:16). This active presence of the Son in the creative work of G_d is revealed fully in the Paschal Mystery, in which Christ, rising as "the first fruits of those who had fallen asleep" (*1 Cor* 15:20), established the new creation and began the process which he himself will bring to completion when he returns in glory to "deliver the kingdom to G_d the Father ..., so that G_d may be everything to everyone" (*1 Cor* 15:24,28).

Already at the dawn of creation, therefore, the plan of G_d implied Christ's "cosmic mission". This *Christocentric perspective*, embracing the whole arc of time, filled G_d's well-pleased gaze when, ceasing from all his work, he "blessed the seventh day and made it holy" (*Gn* 2:3). According to the Priestly writer of the first biblical creation story, then was born the "Sabbath", so characteristic of the first Covenant, and which in some ways foretells the sacred day of the new and final Covenant. The theme of "G_d's rest" (cf. *Gn* 2:2) and the rest which he offered to the people of the Exodus when they entered the Promised Land (cf. *Ex* 33:14; *Dt* 3:20; 12:9; *Jos* 21:44; *Ps* 95:11) is re-read in the New Testament in the light of the definitive "Sabbath rest" (*Heb* 4:9) into which Christ himself has entered by his Resurrection. The People of G_d are called to enter into this same rest by persevering in Christ's example of filial obedience (cf. *Heb* 4:3-16). In order to grasp fully the meaning of Sunday, therefore, we must re-read the great story of creation and deepen our understanding of the theology of the "Sabbath".

"*In the beginning, G_d created the heavens and the earth*" (*Gn* 1:1)

9. The poetic style of the Genesis story conveys well the awe which people feel before the immensity of creation and the resulting sense of adoration of the One who brought all things into being from nothing. It is a story of intense religious significance, a hymn to the Creator of the universe, pointing to him as the only Lord in the face of recurring temptations to divinize the world itself. At the same time, it is a hymn to the goodness of creation, all fashioned by the mighty and merciful hand of G_d.

"G_d saw that it was good" (*Gn* 1:10,12, etc.). Punctuating the story as it does, this refrain *sheds a positive light upon every element of the universe* and reveals the secret for a proper understanding of it and for its eventual regeneration: the world is good insofar as it remains tied to its origin and, after being disfigured by sin, it is again made good when, with the help of grace, it returns to the One who made it. It is clear that this process directly concerns not inanimate objects and animals but human beings, who have been endowed with the incomparable gift and risk of freedom. Immediately after the creation stories, the Bible highlights the dramatic contrast between the grandeur of man, created in the image and likeness of G_d, and the fall of man, which unleashes on the world the darkness of sin and death (cf. *Gn* 3).

10. Coming as it does from the hand of G_d, the cosmos bears the imprint of his goodness. It is a beautiful world, rightly moving us to admiration and delight, but also calling for cultivation and development. At the "completion" of G_d's work, the world is ready for human activity. "On the seventh day G_d finished his work which he had done, and he rested on the seventh day from all his work which he had

done" (*Gn* 2:2). With this anthropomorphic image of G_d's "work", the Bible not only gives us a glimpse of the mysterious relationship between the Creator and the created world, but also casts light upon the task of human beings in relation to the cosmos. The "work" of G_d is in some ways an exemple for man, called not only to inhabit the cosmos, but also to "build" it and thus become G_d's "co-worker". As I wrote in my Encyclical *Laborem Exercens*, the first chapters of Genesis constitute in a sense the first "gospel of work". (10) This is a truth which the Second Vatican Council also stressed: "Created in G_d's image, man was commissioned to subdue the earth and all it contains, to rule the world in justice and holiness, and, recognizing G_d as the creator of all things, to refer himself and the totality of things to G_d so that with everything subject to G_d, the divine name would be glorified in all the earth".(11)

The exhilarating advance of science, technology and culture in their various forms — an ever more rapid and today even overwhelming development — is the historical consequence of the mission by which G_d entrusts to man and woman the task and responsibility of filling the earth and subduing it by means of their work, in the observance of G_d's Law.

"Shabbat": the Creator's joyful rest

11. If the first page of the Book of Genesis presents G_d's "work" as an exemple for man, the same is true of G_d's "rest":"On the seventh day G_d finished his work which he had done" (*Gn* 2:2). Here too we find an anthropomorphism charged with a wealth of meaning.

It would be banal to interpret G_d's "rest" as a kind of divine "inactivity". By its nature, the creative act which founds the world is unceasing and G_d is always at work, as Jesus himself declares in speaking of the

Sabbath precept: "My Father is working still, and I am working" (*Jn* 5:17). The divine rest of the seventh day does not allude to an inactive G_d, but emphasizes the fullness of what has been accomplished. It speaks, as it were, of G_d's lingering before the "very good" work (*Gn* 1:31) which his hand has wrought, in order to cast upon it *a gaze full of joyous delight*. This is a "contemplative" gaze which does not look to new accomplishments but enjoys the beauty of what has already been achieved. It is a gaze which G_d casts upon all things, but in a special way upon man, the crown of creation. It is a gaze which already discloses something of the nuptial shape of the relationship which G_d wants to establish with the creature made in his own image, by calling that creature to enter a pact of love. This is what G_d will gradually accomplish, in offering salvation to all humanity through the saving covenant made with Israel and fulfilled in Christ. It will be the Word Incarnate, through the eschatological gift of the Holy Spirit and the configuration of the Church as his Body and Bride, who will extend to all humanity the offer of mercy and the call of the Father's love.

12. In the Creator's plan, there is both a distinction and a close link between the order of creation and the order

of salvation. This is emphasized in the Old Testament, when it links the "*shabbat*" commandment not only with G_d's mysterious "rest" after the days of creation (cf. *Ex* 20:8-11), but also with the salvation which he offers to Israel *in the liberation from the slavery of Egypt* (cf. *Dt* 5:12-15). The G_d who rests on the seventh day, rejoicing in his creation, is the same G_d who reveals his glory in liberating his children from Pharaoh's oppression. Adopting an image dear to the Prophets, one could say that in both cases *G_d reveals himself as the bridegroom before the bride* (cf. *Hos* 2:16-24; *Jer* 2:2; *Is* 54:4-8).

As certain elements of the same Jewish tradition suggest,(12) to reach the heart of the "*shabbat*", of G_d's "rest", we need to recognize in both the Old and the New Testament the nuptial intensity which marks the relationship between G_d and his people. Hosea, for instance, puts it thus in this marvellous passage: "I will make for you a covenant on that day with the beasts of the field, the birds of the air, and the creeping things of the ground; and I will abolish the bow, the sword, and war from the land; and I will make you lie down in safety. And I will betroth you to me for ever; I will betroth you to me in righteousness and in justice, in steadfast love and in mercy. I will betroth you to me in faithfulness; and you shall know the Lord" (2:18-20).

"G_d blessed the seventh day and made it holy" (Gn 2:3)

13. The Sabbath precept, which in the first Covenant prepares for the Sunday of the new and eternal Covenant, is therefore rooted in the depths of G_d's plan. This is why, unlike many other precepts, it is set not within the context of strictly cultic stipulations but within the Decalogue, the "ten words" which represent the very pillars of the moral life inscribed on the human heart. In setting this commandment within the context of the basic structure of ethics, Israel and then the Church declare that they consider it not just a matter of community religious discipline but *a defining and indelible expression of our relationship with G_d*, announced and expounded by biblical revelation. This is the perspective within which Christians need to rediscover this precept today. Although the precept may merge naturally with the human need for rest, it is faith alone which gives access to its deeper meaning and ensures that it will not become banal and trivialized.

14. In the first place, therefore, Sunday is the day of rest because it is the day "blessed" by G_d and "made holy" by him, set apart from the other days to be, among all of them, "the Lord's Day".

In order to grasp fully what the first of the biblical creation accounts means by keeping the Sabbath "holy", we need to consider the whole story, which shows clearly how every reality, without exception, must be referred back to G_d. Time and space belong to him. He is not the G_d of one day alone, but the G_d of all the days of humanity.

Therefore, if G_d "sanctifies" the seventh day with a special blessing and makes it "his day" *par excellence*, this must be understood within the deep dynamic of the dialogue of the Covenant, indeed the dialogue of "marriage". This is the dialogue of love which knows no interruption, yet is never monotonous. In fact, it employs the different registers of love, from the ordinary and indirect to those more intense, which the words of Scripture and the witness of so many mystics do not hesitate to describe in imagery drawn from the experience of married love.

15. All human life, and therefore all human time, must become praise of the Creator and thanksgiving to him. But man's relationship with G_d also *demands times of explicit prayer*, in which the relationship becomes an intense dialogue, involving every dimension of the person. "The Lord's Day" is the day of this relationship *par excellence* when men and women raise their song to G_d and become the voice of all creation.

This is precisely why it is also *the day of rest*. Speaking vividly as it does of "renewal" and "detachment", the interruption of the often oppressive rhythm of work expresses the dependence of man and the cosmos upon G_d. *Everything belongs to G_d!* The Lord's Day returns again and again to declare this principle within the weekly reckoning of time. The "Sabbath" has therefore been interpreted evocatively as a determining element in the kind of "sacred architecture" of time which marks biblical revelation.(13) It recalls that *the universe and history belong to G_d*; and without a constant awareness of that truth, man cannot serve in the world as co-worker of the Creator.

To "keep holy" by "remembering"

16. The commandment of the Decalogue by which G_d decrees the Sabbath observance is formulated in the Book of Exodus in a distinctive way: "Remember the Sabbath day in order to keep it holy" (20:8). And the inspired text goes on to give the reason for this, recalling as it does the work of G_d: "For in six days the Lord made heaven and earth, the sea, and all that is in them, and rested on the seventh day; therefore the Lord blessed the Sabbath day and made it holy" (v. 11). Before decreeing that something be *done*, the commandment urges that something be *remembered*. It is a call to awaken remembrance of the grand and fundamental work of G_d which is creation, a remembrance which must inspire the entire religious life of man and then fill the day on which man is called

to *rest*. Rest therefore acquires a sacred value: the faithful are called to rest not only *as* G_d rested, but to rest *in* the Lord, bringing the entire creation to him, in praise and thanksgiving, intimate as a child and friendly as a spouse.

17. The connection between Sabbath rest and the theme of "remembering" G_d's wonders is found also in the Book of Deuteronomy (5:12-15), where the precept is grounded less in the work of creation than in the work of liberation accomplished by G_d in the Exodus: "You shall remember that you were a slave in the land of Egypt, and the Lord your G_d brought you out from there with mighty hand and outstretched arm; therefore the Lord your G_d commanded you to keep the Sabbath day" (*Dt* 5:15).

This formulation complements the one we have already seen; and taken together, the two reveal the meaning of "the Lord's Day" within a single theological vision which fuses creation and salvation. Therefore, the main point of the precept is not just any kind of *interruption* of work, but the *celebration* of the marvels which G_d has wrought.

Insofar as this "remembrance" is alive, *full of thanksgiving and of the praise of G_d*, human rest on the Lord's Day takes on its full meaning. It is then that man enters the depths of G_d's "rest" and can experience a tremor of the Creator's joy when, after the creation, he saw that all he had made "was very good" (*Gn* 1:31).

From the Sabbath to Sunday

18. Because the Third Commandment depends upon the remembrance of G_d's saving works and because Christians saw the definitive time inaugurated by Christ as a new beginning, they made the first day after the Sabbath a festive day, for that was the day on which the Lord rose from the dead. The Paschal Mystery of Christ is the full revelation of the mystery of the world's origin, the climax of the history of salvation and the anticipation of the eschatological fulfilment of the world. What G_d accomplished in Creation and wrought for his People in the Exodus has found its fullest expression in Christ's Death and Resurrection, though its definitive fulfilment will not come until the *Parousia*, when Christ returns in glory. In him, the

"spiritual" meaning of the Sabbath is fully realized, as Saint Gregory the Great declares: "For us, the true Sabbath is the person of our Redeemer, our Lord Jesus Christ".(14) This is why the joy with which G_d, on humanity's first Sabbath, contemplates all that was created from nothing, is now expressed in the joy with which Christ, on Easter Sunday, appeared to his disciples, bringing the gift of peace and the gift of the Spirit (cf. *Jn* 20:19-23). It was in the Paschal Mystery that humanity, and with it the whole creation, "groaning in birth-pangs until now" (*Rom* 8:22), came to know its new "exodus" into the freedom of G_d's children who can cry out with Christ, "Abba, Father!" (*Rom* 8:15; *Gal* 4:6). In the light of this mystery, the meaning of the Old Testament precept concerning the Lord's Day is recovered, perfected and fully revealed in the glory which shines on the face of the Risen Christ (cf. *2 Cor* 4:6). We move from the "Sabbath" to the "first day after the Sabbath", from the seventh day to the first day: the *dies Domini* becomes the *dies Christi*!

DIES CHRISTI

CHAPTER II

The Day of the Risen Lord and of the Gift of the Holy Spirit

The weekly Easter

19. "We celebrate Sunday because of the venerable Resurrection of our Lord Jesus Christ, and we do so not only at Easter but also at each turning of the week": so wrote Pope Innocent I at the beginning of the fifth century,(15) testifying to an already well established practice which had evolved from the early years after the Lord's Resurrection. Saint Basil speaks of "holy Sunday, honoured by the Lord's Resurrection, the first fruits of all the other days";(16) and Saint Augustine calls Sunday "a sacrament of

Easter".(17)

The intimate bond between Sunday and the Resurrection of the Lord is strongly emphasized by all the Churches of East and West. In the tradition of the Eastern Churches in particular, every Sunday is the *anastàsimos hemèra*, the day of Resurrection,(18) and this is why it stands at the heart of all worship.

In the light of this constant and universal tradition, it is clear that, although the Lord's Day is rooted in the very work of creation and even more in the mystery of the biblical "rest" of G_d, it is nonetheless to the Resurrection of Christ that we must look in order to understand fully the Lord's Day. This is what the Christian Sunday does, leading the faithful each week to ponder and live the event of Easter, true source of the world's salvation.

20. According to the common witness of the Gospels, the Resurrection of Jesus Christ from the dead took place on "the first day after the Sabbath" (*Mk* 16:2,9; *Lk* 24:1; *Jn* 20:1). On the same day, the Risen Lord

appeared to the two disciples of Emmaus (cf. *Lk* 24:13-35) and to the eleven Apostles gathered together (cf. *Lk* 24:36; *Jn* 20:19). A week later — as the Gospel of John recounts (cf. 20:26) — the disciples were gathered together once again, when Jesus appeared to them and made himself known to Thomas by showing him the signs of his Passion. The day of Pentecost — the first day of the eighth week after the Jewish Passover (cf. *Acts* 2:1), when the promise made by Jesus to the Apostles after the Resurrection was fulfilled by the outpouring of the Holy Spirit (cf. *Lk* 24:49; *Acts* 1:4-5) — also fell on a Sunday. This was the day of the first proclamation and the first baptisms: Peter announced to the assembled crowd that Christ was risen and "those who received his word were baptized" (*Acts* 2:41). This was the epiphany of the Church, revealed as the people into which are gathered in unity, beyond all their differences, the scattered children of G_d.

The first day of the week

21. It was for this reason that, from Apostolic times, "the first day after the Sabbath", the first day of the week, began to shape the rhythm of life for Christ's

disciples (cf. *1 Cor* 16:2). "The first day after the Sabbath" was also the day upon which the faithful of Troas were gathered "for the breaking of bread", when Paul bade them farewell and miraculously restored the young Eutychus to life (cf. *Acts* 20:7-12). The Book of Revelation gives evidence of the practice of calling the first day of the week "the Lord's Day" (1:10). This would now be a characteristic distinguishing Christians from the world around them. As early as the beginning of the second century, it was noted by Pliny the Younger, governor of Bithynia, in his report on the Christian practice "of gathering together on a set day before sunrise and singing among themselves a hymn to Christ as to a G_d".(19) And when Christians spoke of the "Lord's Day", they did so giving to this term the full sense of the Easter proclamation: "Jesus Christ is Lord" (*Phil* 2:11; cf. *Acts* 2:36; *1 Cor* 12:3). Thus Christ was given the same title which the Septuagint used to translate what in the revelation of the Old Testament was the unutterable name of G_d: YHWH.

22. In those early Christian times, the weekly rhythm of days was generally not part of life in the regions where the Gospel spread, and the festive days of the Greek and Roman calendars did not coincide with the Christian

Sunday. For Christians, therefore, it was very difficult to observe the Lord's Day on a set day each week. This explains why the faithful had to gather before sunrise. (20) Yet fidelity to the weekly rhythm became the norm, since it was based upon the New Testament and was tied to Old Testament revelation. This is eagerly underscored by the Apologists and the Fathers of the Church in their writings and preaching where, in speaking of the Paschal Mystery, they use the same Scriptural texts which, according to the witness of Saint Luke (cf. 24:27, 44-47), the Risen Christ himself would have explained to the disciples. In the light of these texts, the celebration of the day of the Resurrection acquired a doctrinal and symbolic value capable of expressing the entire Christian mystery in all its newness.

Growing distinction from the Sabbath

23. It was this newness which the catechesis of the first centuries stressed as it sought to show the prominence of Sunday relative to the Jewish Sabbath. It was on the Sabbath that the Jewish people had to gather in the synagogue and to rest in the way prescribed by the Law.

The Apostles, and in particular Saint Paul, continued initially to attend the synagogue so that there they might proclaim Jesus Christ, commenting upon "the words of the prophets which are read every Sabbath" (*Acts* 13:27). Some communities observed the Sabbath while also celebrating Sunday. Soon, however, the two days began to be distinguished ever more clearly, in reaction chiefly to the insistence of those Christians whose origins in Judaism made them inclined to maintain the obligation of the old Law. Saint Ignatius of Antioch writes: "If those who were living in the former state of things have come to a new hope, no longer observing the Sabbath but keeping the Lord's Day, the day on which our life has appeared through him and his death ..., that mystery from which we have received our faith and in which we persevere in order to be judged disciples of Christ, our only Master, how could we then live without him, given that the prophets too, as his disciples in the Spirit, awaited him as master?".(21) Saint Augustine notes in turn: "Therefore the Lord too has placed his seal on his day, which is the third after the Passion. In the weekly cycle, however, it is the eighth day after the seventh, that is after the Sabbath, and the first day of the week".(22) The distinction of Sunday from the Jewish Sabbath grew ever stronger in the mind of the Church, even though there have been times in history when, because the obligation of Sunday rest was so emphasized, the Lord's Day tended to become more like the Sabbath. Moreover, there have always been groups within Christianity which observe both the Sabbath and Sunday as "two brother days".(23)

The day of the new creation

24. A comparison of the Christian Sunday with the Old Testament vision of the Sabbath prompted theological insights of great interest. In particular, there emerged the unique connection between the Resurrection and Creation. Christian thought spontaneously linked the Resurrection, which took place on "the first day of the week", with the first day of that cosmic week (cf. *Gn* 1:1 - 2:4) which shapes the creation story in the Book of Genesis: the day of the creation of light (cf. 1:3-5). This link invited an understanding of the Resurrection as the beginning of a new creation, the first fruits of which is the glorious Christ, "the first born of all creation" (*Col* 1:15) and "the first born from the dead" (*Col* 1:18).

25. In effect, Sunday is the day above all other days which summons Christians to remember the salvation which was given to them in baptism and which has made them new in Christ. "You were buried with him in baptism, in which you were also raised with him through faith in the working of G_d, who raised him from the dead" (*Col* 2:12; cf. *Rom* 6:4-6). The liturgy underscores this baptismal dimension of Sunday, both in calling for the celebration of baptisms — as well as at the Easter Vigil — on the day of the week "when the Church commemorates the Lord's Resurrection",(24) and in suggesting as an appropriate penitential rite at the start of Mass the sprinkling of holy water, which recalls the moment of Baptism in which all Christian life is born.(25)

The eighth day: image of eternity

26. By contrast, the Sabbath's position as the seventh day of the week suggests for the Lord's Day a complementary symbolism, much loved by the Fathers. Sunday is not only the first day, it is also "the eighth day", set within the sevenfold succession of days in a unique and

transcendent position which evokes not only the beginning of time but also its end in "the age to come". Saint Basil explains that Sunday symbolizes that truly singular day which will follow the present time, the day without end which will know neither evening nor morning, the imperishable age which will never grow old; Sunday is the ceaseless foretelling of life without end which renews the hope of Christians and encourages them on their way. (26) Looking towards the last day, which fulfils completely the eschatological symbolism of the Sabbath, Saint Augustine concludes the Confessions describing the *Eschaton* as "the peace of quietness, the peace of the Sabbath, a peace with no evening".(27) In celebrating Sunday, both the "first" and the "eighth" day, the Christian is led towards the goal of eternal life. (28)

The day of Christ-Light

27. This Christocentric vision sheds light upon another symbolism which Christian reflection and pastoral

practice ascribed to the Lord's Day. Wise pastoral intuition suggested to the Church the christianization of the notion of Sunday as "the day of the sun", which was the Roman name for the day and which is retained in some modern languages.(29) This was in order to draw the faithful away from the seduction of cults which worshipped the sun, and to direct the celebration of the day to Christ, humanity's true "sun". Writing to the pagans, Saint Justin uses the language of the time to note that Christians gather together "on the day named after the sun",(30) but for believers the expression had already assumed a new meaning which was unmistakeably rooted in the Gospel.(31) Christ is the light of the world (cf. *Jn* 9:5; also 1:4-5, 9), and, in the weekly reckoning of time, the day commemorating his Resurrection is the enduring reflection of the epiphany of his glory. The theme of Sunday as the day illuminated by the triumph of the Risen Christ is also found in the Liturgy of the Hours(32) and is given special emphasis in the *Pannichida*, the vigil which in the Eastern liturgies prepares for Sunday. From generation to generation as she gathers on this day, the Church makes her own the wonderment of Zechariah as he looked upon Christ, seeing in him the dawn which gives "light to those who sit in darkness and in the shadow of death" (*Lk* 1:78-79), and she echoes the joy of Simeon when he takes in his arms the divine Child who has come as the "light to enlighten the Gentiles" (*Lk* 2:32).

The day of the gift of the Spirit

28. Sunday, the day of light, could also be called the day of "fire", in reference to the Holy Spirit. The light of Christ is intimately linked to the "fire" of the Spirit, and the two images together reveal the meaning of the Christian Sunday.(33) When he appeared to the Apostles on the evening of Easter, Jesus breathed upon them and said: "Receive the Holy Spirit. If you forgive the sins of any, they are forgiven; if you retain the sins of any, they are retained" (*Jn* 20:22-23). The outpouring of the Spirit was the great gift of the Risen Lord to his disciples on Easter Sunday. It was again Sunday when, fifty days after the Resurrection, the Spirit descended in power, as "a mighty wind" and "fire" (*Acts* 2:2-3), upon the Apostles gathered with Mary. Pentecost is not only the founding event of the Church, but is also the mystery which for ever gives life to the Church.(34) Such an event has its own powerful liturgical moment in the annual celebration which concludes "the great

Sunday",(35) but it also remains a part of the deep meaning of every Sunday, because of its intimate bond with the Paschal Mystery. The "weekly Easter" thus becomes, in a sense, the "weekly Pentecost", when Christians relive the Apostles' joyful encounter with the Risen Lord and receive the life-giving breath of his Spirit.

The day of faith

29. Given these different dimensions which set it apart, Sunday appears as the supreme *day of faith*. It is the day when, by the power of the Holy Spirit, who is the Church's living "memory" (cf. *Jn* 14:26), the first appearance of the Risen Lord becomes an event renewed in the "today" of each of Christ's disciples. Gathered in his presence in the Sunday assembly, believers sense themselves called like the Apostle Thomas: "Put your finger here, and see my hands. Put out your hand, and place it in my side. Doubt no longer, but believe" (*Jn* 20:27). Yes, Sunday is the day of faith. This is stressed by the fact that the Sunday Eucharistic liturgy, like the liturgy of other solemnities, includes the Profession of Faith. Recited or sung, the Creed declares

the baptismal and Paschal character of Sunday, making it the day on which in a special way the baptized renew their adherence to Christ and his Gospel in a rekindled awareness of their baptismal promises. Listening to the word and receiving the Body of the Lord, the baptized contemplate the Risen Jesus present in the "holy signs" and confess with the Apostle Thomas: "My Lord and my G_d!" (*Jn* 20:28).

An indispensable day!

30. It is clear then why, even in our own difficult times, the identity of this day must be protected and above all must be lived in all its depth. An Eastern writer of the beginning of the third century recounts that as early as then the faithful in every region were keeping Sunday holy on a regular basis.(36) What began as a spontaneous practice later became a juridically sanctioned norm. The Lord's Day has structured the history of the Church through two thousand years: how could we think that it will not continue to shape her future? The pressures of today can make it harder to fulfil the Sunday obligation; and, with a mother's sensitivity, the Church looks to the circumstances of

each of her children. In particular, she feels herself called to a new catechetical and pastoral commitment, in order to ensure that, in the normal course of life, none of her children are deprived of the rich outpouring of grace which the celebration of the Lord's Day brings. It was in this spirit that the Second Vatican Council, making a pronouncement on the possibility of reforming the Church calendar to match different civil calendars, declared that the Church "is prepared to accept only those arrangements which preserve a week of seven days with a Sunday".(37) Given its many meanings and aspects, and its link to the very foundations of the faith, the celebration of the Christian Sunday remains, on the threshold of the Third Millennium, an indispensable element of our Christian identity.

DIES ECCLESIAE

CHAPTER III

The Eucharistic Assembly:
Heart of Sunday

The presence of the Risen Lord

31. "I am with you always, to the end of the age" (*Mt* 28:20). This promise of Christ never ceases to resound in the Church as the fertile secret of her life and the wellspring of her hope. As the day of Resurrection, Sunday is not only the remembrance of a past event: it is a celebration of the living presence of the Risen Lord in the midst of his own people.

For this presence to be properly proclaimed and lived, it is not enough that the disciples of Christ pray individually and commemorate the death and Resurrection of Christ inwardly, in the secrecy of their hearts. Those who have received the grace of baptism are not saved as individuals alone, but as members of the Mystical Body, having become part of the People of G_d.(38) It is important therefore that they come together to express fully the very identity of the Church, the *ekklesia*, the assembly called together by the Risen Lord who offered his life "to reunite the scattered children of G_d" (*Jn* 11:52). They have become "one" in Christ (cf. *Gal* 3:28) through the gift of the Spirit. This unity becomes visible when Christians gather together: it is then that they come to know vividly and to testify to the world that they are the people redeemed, drawn "from every tribe and language and people and nation" (*Rev* 5:9). The assembly of Christ's disciples embodies from age to age the image of the first Christian community which Luke gives as an example in the Acts of the Apostles, when he recounts that the first baptized believers "devoted themselves to the apostles' teaching and fellowship, to the breaking of bread and the prayers" (2:42).

The Eucharistic assembly

32. The Eucharist is not only a particularly intense expression of the reality of the Church's life, but also in a sense its "fountain-head".(39) The Eucharist feeds and forms the Church: "Because there is one bread, we who are many are one body, for we all partake of the one bread" (*1 Cor* 10:17). Because of this vital link with the sacrament of the Body and Blood of the Lord, the mystery of the Church is savoured, proclaimed, and lived supremely in the Eucharist.(40)

This ecclesial dimension intrinsic to the Eucharist is realized in every Eucharistic celebration. But it is expressed most especially on the day when the whole community comes together to commemorate the Lord's Resurrection. Significantly, the Catechism of the Catholic Church teaches that "the Sunday celebration of the Lord's Day and his Eucharist is at the heart of the Church's life".(41)

33. At Sunday Mass, Christians relive with particular intensity the experience of the Apostles on the evening of Easter when the Risen Lord appeared to them as they were gathered together (cf. *Jn* 20:19). In a sense, the People of G_d of all times were present in that small

nucleus of disciples, the first fruits of the Church. Through their testimony, every generation of believers hears the greeting of Christ, rich with the messianic gift of peace, won by his blood and offered with his Spirit: "Peace be with you!" Christ's return among them "a week later" (*Jn* 20:26) can be seen as a radical prefiguring of the Christian community's practice of coming together every seven days, on "the Lord's Day" or Sunday, in order to profess faith in his Resurrection and to receive the blessing which he had promised: "Blessed are those who have not seen and yet believe" (*Jn* 20:29). This close connection between the appearance of the Risen Lord and the Eucharist is suggested in the Gospel of Luke in the story of the two disciples of Emmaus, whom Christ approached and led to understand the Scriptures and then sat with them at table. They recognized him when he "took the bread, said the blessing, broke it and gave it to them" (24:30). The gestures of Jesus in this account are his gestures at the Last Supper, with the clear allusion to the "breaking of bread", as the Eucharist was called by the first generation of Christians.

The Sunday Eucharist

34. It is true that, in itself, the Sunday Eucharist is no different from the Eucharist celebrated on other days, nor can it be separated from liturgical and sacramental life as a whole. By its very nature, the Eucharist is an epiphany of the Church;(42) and this is most powerfully expressed when the diocesan community gathers in prayer with its Pastor: "The Church appears with special clarity when the holy People of G_d, all of them, are actively and fully sharing in the same liturgical celebrations — especially when it is the same Eucharist — sharing one prayer at one altar, at which the Bishop is presiding, surrounded by his presbyters and his ministers".(43) This relationship with the Bishop and with the entire Church community is inherent in every Eucharistic celebration, even when the Bishop does not preside, regardless of the day of the week on which it is celebrated. The mention of the Bishop in the Eucharistic Prayer is the indication of this.

But because of its special solemnity and the obligatory presence of the community, and because it is celebrated "on the day when Christ conquered death and gave us a share in his immortal life",(44) the Sunday Eucharist expresses with greater emphasis its inherent ecclesial dimension. It becomes the paradigm for other

Eucharistic celebrations. Each community, gathering all its members for the "breaking of the bread", becomes the place where the mystery of the Church is concretely made present. In celebrating the Eucharist, the community opens itself to communion with the universal Church,(45) imploring the Father to "remember the Church throughout the world" and make her grow in the unity of all the faithful with the Pope and with the Pastors of the particular Churches, until love is brought to perfection.

The day of the Church

35. Therefore, the *dies Domini* is also the *dies Ecclesiae*. This is why on the pastoral level the community aspect of the Sunday celebration should be particularly stressed. As I have noted elsewhere, among the many activities of a parish, "none is as vital or as community-forming as the Sunday celebration of the Lord's Day and his Eucharist".(46) Mindful of this, the Second Vatican Council recalled that efforts must be made to ensure that there is "within the parish, a lively sense of community, in the first place through the community celebration of Sunday Mass".(47)

Subsequent liturgical directives made the same point, asking that on Sundays and holy days the Eucharistic celebrations held normally in other churches and chapels be coordinated with the celebration in the parish church, in order "to foster the sense of the Church community, which is nourished and expressed in a particular way by the community celebration on Sunday, whether around the Bishop, especially in the Cathedral, or in the parish assembly, in which the pastor represents the Bishop".(48)

36. The Sunday assembly is the privileged place of unity: it is the setting for the celebration of the *sacramentum unitatis* which profoundly marks the Church as a people gathered "by" and "in" the unity of the Father, of the Son and of the Holy Spirit.(49) For Christian families, the Sunday assembly is one of the most outstanding expressions of their identity and their "ministry" as "domestic churches",(50) when parents share with their children at the one Table of the word and of the Bread of Life. We do well to recall in this regard that it is first of all the parents who must teach their children to participate in Sunday Mass; they are assisted in this by catechists, who are to see to it that initiation into the Mass is made a part of the formation

imparted to the children entrusted to their care, explaining the important reasons behind the obligatory nature of the precept. When circumstances suggest it, the celebration of Masses for Children, in keeping with the provisions of the liturgical norms,(51) can also help in this regard.

At Sunday Masses in parishes, insofar as parishes are "Eucharistic communities",(52) it is normal to find different groups, movements, associations and even the smaller religious communities present in the parish. This allows everyone to experience in common what they share most deeply, beyond the particular spiritual paths which, by discernment of Church authority,(53) legitimately distinguish them. This is why on Sunday, the day of gathering, small group Masses are not to be encouraged: it is not only a question of ensuring that parish assemblies are not without the necessary ministry of priests, but also of ensuring that the life and unity of the Church community are fully safeguarded and promoted.(54) Authorization of possible and clearly restricted exceptions to this general guideline will depend upon the wise discernment of the Pastors of the particular Churches, in view of special needs in the area of formation and pastoral care, and keeping in mind the good of individuals or groups — especially the benefits which such exceptions may bring to the entire Christian community.

A pilgrim people

37. As the Church journeys through time, the reference to Christ's Resurrection and the weekly recurrence of this solemn memorial help to remind us of *the pilgrim and eschatological character of the People of G_d.* Sunday after Sunday the Church moves towards the final "Lord's Day", that Sunday which knows no end. The expectation of Christ's coming is inscribed in the very mystery of the Church(55) and is evidenced in every Eucharistic celebration. But, with its specific remembrance of the glory of the Risen Christ, the Lord's Day recalls with greater intensity the future glory of his "return". This makes Sunday the day on which the Church, showing forth more clearly her identity as "Bride", anticipates in some sense the eschatological reality of the heavenly Jerusalem. Gathering her children into the Eucharistic assembly and teaching them to wait for the "divine Bridegroom", she engages in a kind of "exercise of desire",(56) receiving a

foretaste of the joy of the new heavens and new earth, when the holy city, the new Jerusalem, will come down from G_d, "prepared as a bride adorned for her husband" (*Rev* 21:2).

The day of hope

38. Viewed in this way, Sunday is not only the day of faith, but is also *the day of Christian hope*. To share in "the Lord's Supper" is to anticipate the eschatological feast of the "marriage of the Lamb" (*Rev* 19:9). Celebrating this memorial of Christ, risen and ascended into heaven, the Christian community waits "in joyful hope for the coming of our Saviour, Jesus Christ".(57) Renewed and nourished by this intense weekly rhythm, Christian hope becomes the leaven and the light of human hope. This is why the Prayer of the Faithful responds not only to the needs of the particular Christian community but also to those of all humanity; and the Church, coming together for the Eucharistic celebration, shows to the world that she makes her own "the joys and hopes, the sorrows and anxieties of people today, especially of the poor and all those who suffer". (58) With the offering of the Sunday Eucharist, the

Church crowns the witness which her children strive to offer every day of the week by proclaiming the Gospel and practising charity in the world of work and in all the many tasks of life; thus she shows forth more plainly her identity "as a sacrament, or sign and instrument of intimate union with G_d and of the unity of the entire human race".(59)

The table of the word

39. As in every Eucharistic celebration, the Risen Lord is encountered in the Sunday assembly at the twofold table of the word and of the Bread of Life. The table of the word offers the same understanding of the history of salvation and especially of the Paschal Mystery which the Risen Jesus himself gave to his disciples: it is Christ who speaks, present as he is in his word "when Sacred Scripture is read in the Church".(60) At the table of the Bread of Life, the Risen Lord becomes really, substantially and enduringly present through the memorial of his Passion and Resurrection, and the Bread of Life is offered as a pledge of future glory. The Second Vatican Council recalled that "the Liturgy of the Word and the Liturgy of the Eucharist are so closely

joined together that they form a single act of worship". (61) The Council also urged that "the table of the word of G_d be more lavishly prepared for the faithful, opening to them more abundantly the treasures of the Bible".(62) It then decreed that, in Masses of Sunday and holy days of obligation, the homily should not be omitted except for serious reasons.(63) These timely decrees were faithfully embodied in the liturgical reform, about which Paul VI wrote, commenting upon the richer offering of biblical readings on Sunday and holy days: "All this has been decreed so as to foster more and more in the faithful 'that hunger for hearing the word of the Lord' (*Am* 8:11) which, under the guidance of the Holy Spirit, spurs the People of the New Covenant on towards the perfect unity of the Church".(64)

40. In considering the Sunday Eucharist more than thirty years after the Council, we need to assess how well the word of G_d is being proclaimed and how effectively the People of G_d have grown in knowledge and love of Sacred Scripture.(65) There are two aspects of this — that of *celebration* and that of *personal appropriation* — and they are very closely related. At the level of celebration, the fact that the Council made it

possible to proclaim the word of G_d in the language of the community taking part in the celebration must awaken a new sense of responsibility towards the word, allowing "the distinctive character of the sacred text" to shine forth "even in the mode of reading or singing". (66) At the level of personal appropriation, the hearing of the word of G_d proclaimed must be well prepared in the souls of the faithful by an apt knowledge of Scripture and, where pastorally possible, by *special initiatives designed to deepen understanding of the biblical readings*, particularly those used on Sundays and holy days. If Christian individuals and families are not regularly drawing new life from the reading of the sacred text in a spirit of prayer and docility to the Church's interpretation,(67) then it is difficult for the liturgical proclamation of the word of G_d alone to produce the fruit we might expect. This is the value of initiatives in parish communities which bring together during the week those who take part in the Eucharist — priest, ministers and faithful(68) — in order to prepare the Sunday liturgy, reflecting beforehand upon the word of G_d which will be proclaimed. The objective sought here is that the entire celebration — praying, singing, listening, and not just the preaching — should express in some way the theme of the Sunday liturgy, so that all those taking part may be penetrated more powerfully by it. Clearly, much depends on those who exercise the ministry of the word. It is their duty to prepare the reflection on the word of the Lord by prayer and study of the sacred text, so that they may then express its contents faithfully and apply them to people's concerns and to their daily lives.

41. It should also be borne in mind that *the liturgical proclamation of the word of G_d*, especially in the Eucharistic assembly, is not so much a time for meditation and catechesis as *a dialogue between G_d and his People*, a dialogue in which the wonders of salvation are proclaimed and the demands of the Covenant are continually restated. On their part, the People of G_d are drawn to respond to this dialogue of love by giving thanks and praise, also by demonstrating their fidelity to the task of continual "conversion". The Sunday assembly commits us therefore to an inner renewal of our baptismal promises, which are in a sense implicit in the recitation of the Creed, and are an explicit part of the liturgy of the Easter Vigil and whenever Baptism is celebrated during Mass. In this context, the proclamation of the word in the Sunday Eucharistic celebration takes on the solemn tone found in the Old Testament at moments when the Covenant

was renewed, when the Law was proclaimed and the community of Israel was called — like the People in the desert at the foot of Sinai (cf. *Ex* 19:7-8; 24:3,7) — to repeats its "yes", renewing its decision to be faithful to G_d and to obey his commandments. In speaking his word, G_d awaits our response: a response which Christ has already made for us with his "Amen" (cf. *2 Cor* 1:20-22), and which echoes in us through the Holy Spirit so that what we hear may involve us at the deepest level.(69)

The table of the Body of Christ

42. The table of the word leads naturally to the table of the Eucharistic Bread and prepares the community to live its many aspects, which in the Sunday Eucharist assume an especially solemn character. As the whole community gathers to celebrate "the Lord's Day", the Eucharist appears more clearly than on other days as the great "thanksgiving" in which the Spirit-filled Church turns to the Father, becoming one with Christ and speaking in the name of all humanity. The rhythm of the week prompts us to gather up in grateful memory the events of the days which have just passed, to review

them in the light of G_d and to thank him for his countless gifts, glorifying him "through Christ, with Christ and in Christ, in the unity of the Holy Spirit". The Christian community thus comes to a renewed awareness of the fact that all things were created through Christ (cf. *Col* 1:16; *Jn* 1:3), and that in Christ, who came in the form of a slave to take on and redeem our human condition, all things have been restored (cf. *Eph* 1:10), in order to be handed over to G_d the Father, from whom all things come to be and draw their life. Then, giving assent to the Eucharistic doxology with their "Amen", the People of G_d look in faith and hope towards the eschatological end, when Christ "will deliver the kingdom to G_d the Father ... so that G_d may be everything to everyone" (*1 Cor* 15:24, 28).

43. This "ascending" movement is inherent in every Eucharistic celebration and makes it a joyous event, overflowing with gratitude and hope. But it emerges particularly at Sunday Mass because of its special link with the commemoration of the Resurrection. By contrast, this "Eucharistic" rejoicing which "lifts up our hearts" is the fruit of G_d's "descending" movement towards us, which remains for ever etched in the essential sacrificial element of the Eucharist, the

supreme expression and celebration of the mystery of the *kenosis*, the descent by which Christ "humbled himself, and became obedient unto death, even death on a Cross" (*Phil* 2:8).

The Mass in fact *truly makes present the sacrifice of the Cross*. Under the species of bread and wine, upon which has been invoked the outpouring of the Spirit who works with absolutely unique power in the words of consecration, Christ offers himself to the Father in the same act of sacrifice by which he offered himself on the Cross. "In this divine sacrifice which is accomplished in the Mass, the same Christ who offered himself once and for all in a bloody manner on the altar of the Cross is contained and is offered in an unbloody manner".(70) To his sacrifice Christ unites the sacrifice of the Church: "In the Eucharist the sacrifice of Christ becomes also the sacrifice of the members of his Body. The lives of the faithful, their praise, sufferings, prayer and work, are united with those of Christ and with his total offering, and so acquire a new value".(71) The truth that the whole community shares in Christ's sacrifice is especially evident in the Sunday gathering, which makes it possible to bring to the altar the week that has passed, with all its human burdens.

Easter banquet and fraternal gathering

44. The communal character of the Eucharist emerges in a special way when it is seen as the Easter banquet, in which Christ himself becomes our nourishment. In fact, "for this purpose Christ entrusted to the Church this sacrifice: so that the faithful might share in it, both spiritually, in faith and charity, and sacramentally, in the banquet of Holy Communion. Sharing in the Lord's Supper is always communion with Christ, who offers himself for us in sacrifice to the Father".(72) This is why the Church *recommends that the faithful receive communion when they take part in the Eucharist*, provided that they are properly disposed and, if aware of grave sin, have received G_d's pardon in the Sacrament of Reconciliation,(73) in the spirit of what Saint Paul writes to the community at Corinth (cf. *1 Cor* 11:27-32). Obviously, the invitation to Eucharistic communion is more insistent in the case of Mass on Sundays and holy days.

It is also important to be ever mindful that communion with Christ is deeply tied to communion with our brothers and sisters. The Sunday Eucharistic gathering is *an experience of brotherhood*, which the celebration should demonstrate clearly, while ever respecting the nature of the liturgical action. All this will be helped by gestures of welcome and by the tone of prayer, alert to the needs of all in the community. The sign of peace — in the Roman Rite significantly placed before Eucharistic communion — is a particularly expressive gesture which the faithful are invited to make as a manifestation of the People of G_d's acceptance of all that has been accomplished in the celebration(74) and of the commitment to mutual love which is made in sharing the one bread, with the demanding words of Christ in mind: "If you are offering your gift at the altar, and there remember that your brother has something against you, leave your gift there before the altar and go; first be reconciled with your brother, and then come and offer your gift" (*Mt* 5:23-24).

From Mass to "mission"

45. Receiving the Bread of Life, the disciples of Christ ready themselves to undertake with the strength of the Risen Lord and his Spirit *the tasks which await them in their ordinary life*. For the faithful who have understood

the meaning of what they have done, the Eucharistic celebration does not stop at the church door. Like the first witnesses of the Resurrection, Christians who gather each Sunday to experience and proclaim the presence of the Risen Lord are called *to evangelize and bear witness* in their daily lives. Given this, the Prayer after Communion and the Concluding Rite — the Final Blessing and the Dismissal — need to be better valued and appreciated, so that all who have shared in the Eucharist may come to a deeper sense of the responsibility which is entrusted to them. Once the assembly disperses, Christ's disciples return to their everyday surroundings with the commitment to make their whole life a gift, a spiritual sacrifice pleasing to G_d (cf. *Rom* 12:1). They feel indebted to their brothers and sisters because of what they have received in the celebration, not unlike the disciples of Emmaus who, once they had recognized the Risen Christ "in the breaking of the bread" (cf. *Lk* 24:30-32), felt the need to return immediately to share with their brothers and sisters the joy of meeting the Lord (cf. *Lk* 24:33-35).

The Sunday obligation

46. Since the Eucharist is the very heart of Sunday, it is clear why, from the earliest centuries, the Pastors of the Church have not ceased to remind the faithful of *the need to take part in the liturgical assembly*. "Leave everything on the Lord's Day", urges the third century text known as the *Didascalia*, "and run diligently to your assembly, because it is your praise of G_d. Otherwise, what excuse will they make to G_d, those who do not come together on the Lord's Day to hear the word of life and feed on the divine nourishment which lasts forever?".(75) The faithful have generally accepted this call of the Pastors with conviction of soul and, although there have been times and situations when this duty has not been perfectly met, one should never forget the genuine heroism of priests and faithful who have fulfilled this obligation even when faced with danger and the denial of religious freedom, as can be documented from the first centuries of Christianity up to our own time.

In his first Apology addressed to the Emperor Antoninus and the Senate, Saint Justin proudly described the Christian practice of the Sunday assembly, which gathered in one place Christians from both the city and the countryside.(76) When, during the persecution of Diocletian, their assemblies were banned with the greatest severity, many were courageous enough to defy the imperial decree and accepted death rather than miss the Sunday Eucharist. This was the case of the martyrs of Abitina, in Proconsular Africa, who replied to their accusers: "Without fear of any kind we have celebrated the Lord's Supper, because it cannot be missed; that is our law"; "We cannot live without the Lord's Supper". As she confessed her faith, one of the martyrs said: "Yes, I went to the assembly and I celebrated the Lord's Supper with my brothers and sisters, because I am a Christian".(77)

47. Even if in the earliest times it was not judged necessary to be prescriptive, the Church has not ceased to confirm this obligation of conscience, which rises from the inner need felt so strongly by the Christians of the first centuries. It was only later, faced with the half-heartedness or negligence of some, that the Church had to make explicit the duty to attend Sunday Mass: more often than not, this was done in the form of exhortation, but at times the Church had to resort to specific canonical precepts. This was the case in a number of local Councils from the fourth century onwards (as at the Council of Elvira of 300, which speaks not of an

obligation but of penalties after three absences)(78) and most especially from the sixth century onwards (as at the Council of Agde in 506).(79) These decrees of local Councils led to a universal practice, the obligatory character of which was taken as something quite normal.(80)

The Code of Canon Law of 1917 for the first time gathered this tradition into a universal law.(81) The present Code reiterates this, saying that "on Sundays and other holy days of obligation the faithful are bound to attend Mass".(82) This legislation has normally been understood as entailing a grave obligation: this is the teaching of the Catechism of the Catholic Church,(83) and it is easy to understand why if we keep in mind how vital Sunday is for the Christian life.

48. Today, as in the heroic times of the beginning, many who wish to live in accord with the demands of their faith are being faced with difficult situations in various parts of the world. They live in surroundings which are sometimes decidedly hostile and at other times — more frequently in fact — indifferent and unresponsive to the Gospel message. If believers are not to be overwhelmed,

they must be able to count on the support of the Christian community. This is why they must be convinced that it is crucially important for the life of faith that they should come together with others on Sundays to celebrate the Passover of the Lord in the sacrament of the New Covenant. It is the special responsibility of the Bishops, therefore, "to ensure that Sunday is appreciated by all the faithful, kept holy and celebrated as truly 'the Lord's Day', on which the Church comes together to renew the remembrance of the Easter mystery in hearing the word of G_d, in offering the sacrifice of the Lord, in keeping the day holy by means of prayer, works of charity and abstention from work".(84)

49. Because the faithful are obliged to attend Mass unless there is a grave impediment, Pastors have the corresponding duty to offer to everyone the real possibility of fulfilling the precept. The provisions of Church law move in this direction, as for example in the faculty granted to priests, with the prior authorization of the diocesan Bishop, to celebrate more than one Mass on Sundays and holy days,(85) the institution of evening Masses(86) and the provision which allows the obligation to be fulfilled from Saturday evening

onwards, starting at the time of First Vespers of Sunday. (87) From a liturgical point of view, in fact, holy days begin with First Vespers.(88) Consequently, the liturgy of what is sometimes called the "Vigil Mass" is in effect the "festive" Mass of Sunday, at which the celebrant is required to preach the homily and recite the Prayer of the Faithful.

Moreover, Pastors should remind the faithful that when they are away from home on Sundays they are to take care to attend Mass wherever they may be, enriching the local community with their personal witness. At the same time, these communities should show a warm sense of welcome to visiting brothers and sisters, especially in places which attract many tourists and pilgrims, for whom it will often be necessary to provide special religious assistance.(89)

A joyful celebration in song

50. Given the nature of Sunday Mass and its importance in the lives of the faithful, it must be prepared with special care. In ways dictated by pastoral experience

and local custom in keeping with liturgical norms, efforts must be made to ensure that the celebration has the festive character appropriate to the day commemorating the Lord's Resurrection. To this end, it is important to devote attention to the *songs used by the assembly*, since singing is a particularly apt way to express a joyful heart, accentuating the solemnity of the celebration and fostering the sense of a common faith and a shared love. Care must be taken to ensure the quality, both of the texts and of the melodies, so that what is proposed today as new and creative will conform to liturgical requirements and be worthy of the Church's tradition which, in the field of sacred music, boasts a priceless heritage.

A celebration involving all

51. There is a need too to ensure that all those present, children and adults, take an active interest, by encouraging their involvement at those points where the liturgy suggests and recommends it.(90) Of course, it falls only to those who exercise the priestly ministry to effect the Eucharistic Sacrifice and to offer it to G_d in the name of the whole people.(91) This is the basis of

the distinction, which is much more than a matter of discipline, between the task proper to the celebrant and that which belongs to deacons and the non-ordained faithful.(92) Yet the faithful must realize that, because of the common priesthood received in Baptism, "they participate in the offering of the Eucharist".(93) Although there is a distinction of roles, they still "offer to G_d the divine victim and themselves with him. Offering the sacrifice and receiving holy communion, they take part actively in the liturgy",(94) finding in it light and strength to live their baptismal priesthood and the witness of a holy life.

Other moments of the Christian Sunday

52. Sharing in the Eucharist is the heart of Sunday, but the duty to keep Sunday holy cannot be reduced to this. In fact, the Lord's Day is lived well if it is marked from beginning to end by grateful and active remembrance of G_d's saving work. This commits each of Christ's disciples to shape the other moments of the day — those outside the liturgical context: family life, social relationships, moments of relaxation — in such a way that the peace and joy of the Risen Lord will emerge in

the ordinary events of life. For example, the relaxed gathering of parents and children can be an opportunity not only to listen to one another but also to share a few formative and more reflective moments. Even in lay life, when possible, why not make provision for special *times of prayer* — especially the solemn celebration of Vespers, for example — or *moments of catechesis*, which on the eve of Sunday or on Sunday afternoon might prepare for or complete the gift of the Eucharist in people's hearts?

This rather traditional way of keeping Sunday holy has perhaps become more difficult for many people; but the Church shows her faith in the strength of the Risen Lord and the power of the Holy Spirit by making it known that, today more than ever, she is unwilling to settle for minimalism and mediocrity at the level of faith. She wants to help Christians to do what is most correct and pleasing to the Lord. And despite the difficulties, there are positive and encouraging signs. In many parts of the Church, a new need for prayer in its many forms is being felt; and this is a gift of the Holy Spirit. There is also a rediscovery of ancient religious practices, such as pilgrimages; and often the faithful take advantage of Sunday rest to visit a Shrine where, with the whole family perhaps, they can spend time in a more intense experience of faith. These are moments of grace which must be fostered through evangelization and guided by genuine pastoral wisdom.

Sunday assemblies without a priest

53. There remains the problem of parishes which do not have the ministry of a priest for the celebration of the Sunday Eucharist. This is often the case in young Churches, where one priest has pastoral responsibility for faithful scattered over a vast area. However, emergency situations can also arise in countries of long-standing Christian tradition, where diminishing numbers of clergy make it impossible to guarantee the presence of a priest in every parish community. In situations where the Eucharist cannot be celebrated, the Church recommends that the Sunday assembly come together even without a priest,(95) in keeping with the indications and directives of the Holy See which have been entrusted to the Episcopal Conferences for implementation.(96) Yet the objective must always remain the celebration of the Sacrifice of the Mass, the one way in which the Passover of the Lord becomes

truly present, the only full realization of the Eucharistic assembly over which the priest presides *in persona Christi*, breaking the bread of the word and the Eucharist. At the pastoral level, therefore, everything has to be done to ensure that the Sacrifice of the Mass is made available as often as possible to the faithful who are regularly deprived of it, either by arranging the presence of a priest from time to time, or by taking every opportunity to organize a gathering in a central location accessible to scattered groups.

Radio and television

54. Finally, the faithful who, because of sickness, disability or some other serious cause, are prevented from taking part, should as best they can unite themselves with the celebration of Sunday Mass from afar, preferably by means of the readings and prayers for that day from the Missal, as well as through their desire for the Eucharist.(97) In many countries, radio and television make it possible to join in the Eucharistic celebration broadcast from some sacred place.(98) Clearly, this kind of broadcast does not in itself fulfil the Sunday obligation, which requires participation in

the fraternal assembly gathered in one place, where Eucharistic communion can be received. But for those who cannot take part in the Eucharist and who are therefore excused from the obligation, radio and television are a precious help, especially if accompanied by the generous service of extraordinary ministers who bring the Eucharist to the sick, also bringing them the greeting and solidarity of the whole community. Sunday Mass thus produces rich fruits for these Christians too, and they are truly enabled to experience Sunday as "the Lord's Day" and "the Church's day".

DIES HOMINIS

CHAPTER IV

Sunday: Day of Joy, Rest and Solidarity

The "full joy" of Christ

55. "Blessed be he who has raised the great day of Sunday above all other days. The heavens and the earth, angels and of men give themselves over to joy".(99) This cry of the Maronite liturgy captures well the intense acclamations of joy which have always characterized Sunday in the liturgy of both East and West. Moreover, historically — even before it was seen as a day of rest, which in any case was not provided for in the civil calendar — Christians celebrated the weekly day of the Risen Lord primarily as a day of joy. "On the first day of the week, you shall all rejoice", urges the *Didascalia.* (100) This was also emphasized by liturgical practice, through the choice of appropriate gestures. (101) Voicing an awareness widespread in the

Church, Saint Augustine describes the joy of the weekly Easter: "Fasting, is set aside and prayers are said standing, as a sign of the Resurrection, which is also why the Alleluia is sung on every Sunday". (102)

56. Beyond particular ritual forms, which can vary in time depending upon Church discipline, there remains the fact that Sunday, as a weekly echo of the first encounter with the Risen Lord, is unfailingly marked by the joy with which the disciples greeted the Master: "The disciples rejoiced to see the Lord" (*Jn* 20:20). This was the confirmation of the words which Jesus spoke before the Passion and which resound in every Christian generation: "You will be sorrowful, but your sorrow will turn to joy" (*Jn* 16:20). Had not he himself prayed for this, that the disciples would have "the fullness of his joy" (cf. *Jn* 17:13)? The festive character of the Sunday Eucharist expresses the joy that Christ communicates to his Church through the gift of the Spirit. Joy is precisely one of the fruits of the Holy Spirit (cf. *Rom* 14:17; *Gal* 5:22).

57. Therefore, if we wish to rediscover the full meaning of Sunday, we must rediscover this aspect of the life of

faith. Certainly, Christian joy must mark the whole of life, and not just one day of the week. But in virtue of its significance as *the day of the Risen Lord*, celebrating G_d's work of creation and "new creation", Sunday is the day of joy in a very special way, indeed the day most suitable for learning how to rejoice and to rediscover the true nature and deep roots of joy. This joy should never be confused with shallow feelings of satisfaction and pleasure, which inebriate the senses and emotions for a brief moment, but then leave the heart unfulfilled and perhaps even embittered. In the Christian view, joy is much more enduring and consoling; as the saints attest, it can hold firm even in the dark night of suffering. (103) It is, in a certain sense, a "virtue" to be nurtured.

58. Yet there is no conflict whatever between Christian joy and true human joys, which in fact are exalted and find their ultimate foundation precisely in the joy of the glorified Christ, the perfect image and revelation of man as G_d intended. As my revered predecessor Paul VI wrote in his Exhortation on Christian joy: "In essence, Christian joy is a sharing in the unfathomable joy, at once divine and human, found in the heart of the glorified Christ". (104) Pope Paul concluded his

Exhortation by asking that, on the Lord's Day, the Church should witness powerfully to the joy experienced by the Apostles when they saw the Lord on the evening of Easter. To this end, he urged pastors to insist "upon the need for the baptized to celebrate the Sunday Eucharist in joy. How could they neglect this encounter, this banquet which Christ prepares for us in his love? May our sharing in it be most worthy and joyful! It is Christ, crucified and glorified, who comes among his disciples, to lead them all together into the newness of his Resurrection. This is the climax, here below, of the covenant of love between G_d and his people: the sign and source of Christian joy, a stage on the way to the eternal feast". (105) This vision of faith shows the Christian Sunday to be a true "time for celebration", a day given by G_d to men and women for their full human and spiritual growth.

The fulfilment of the Sabbath

59. This aspect of the Christian Sunday shows in a special way how it is the fulfilment of the Old Testament Sabbath. On the Lord's Day, which — as we have already said — the Old Testament links to the

work of creation (cf. *Gn* 2:1-3; *Ex* 20:8-11) and the Exodus (cf. *Dt* 5:12-15), the Christian is called to proclaim the new creation and the new covenant brought about in the Paschal Mystery of Christ. Far from being abolished, the celebration of creation becomes more profound within a Christocentric perspective, being seen in the light of the G_d's plan "to unite all things in [Christ], things in heaven and things on earth" (*Eph* 1:10). The remembrance of the liberation of the Exodus also assumes its full meaning as it becomes a remembrance of the universal redemption accomplished by Christ in his Death and Resurrection. More than a "replacement" for the Sabbath, therefore, Sunday is its fulfilment, and in a certain sense its extension and full expression in the ordered unfolding of the history of salvation, which reaches its culmination in Christ.

60. In this perspective, the biblical theology of the "Sabbath" can be recovered in full, without compromising the Christian character of Sunday. It is a theology which leads us ever anew and in unfailing awe to the mystery of the beginning, when the eternal Word of G_d, by a free decision of love, created the world from nothing. The work of creation was sealed by the

blessing and consecration of the day on which G_d ceased "from all the work which he had done in creation" (*Gn* 2:3). This day of G_d's rest confers meaning upon time, which in the sequence of weeks assumes not only a chronological regularity but also, in a manner of speaking, a theological resonance. The constant return of the "*shabbat*" ensures that there is no risk of time being closed in upon itself, since, in welcoming G_d and his *kairoi* — the moments of his grace and his saving acts — time remains open to eternity.

61. As the seventh day blessed and consecrated by G_d, the "shabbat" concludes the whole work of creation, and is therefore immediately linked to the work of the sixth day when G_d made man "in his image and likeness" (cf. *Gn* 1:26). This very close connection between the "day of G_d" and the "day of man" did not escape the Fathers in their meditation on the biblical creation story. Saint Ambrose says in this regard: "Thanks, then, to the Lord our G_d who accomplished a work in which he might find rest. He made the heavens, but I do not read that he found rest there; he made the stars, the moon, the sun, and neither do I read that he found rest in them. I read instead that he made man and

that then he rested, finding in man one to whom he could offer the forgiveness of sins". (106) Thus there will be for ever a direct link between the "day of G_d" and the "day of man". When the divine commandment declares: "Remember the Sabbath day in order to keep it holy" (*Ex* 20:8), the rest decreed in order to honour the day dedicated to G_d is not at all a burden imposed upon man, but rather an aid to help him to recognize his life-giving and liberating dependence upon the Creator, and at the same time his calling to cooperate in the Creator's work and to receive his grace. In honouring G_d's "rest", man fully discovers himself, and thus the Lord's Day bears the profound imprint of G_d's blessing (cf. *Gn* 2:3), by virtue of which, we might say, it is endowed in a way similar to the animals and to man himself, with a kind of "fruitfulness" (cf. *Gn* 1:22, 28). This "fruitfulness" is apparent above all in filling and, in a certain sense, "multiplying" time itself, deepening in men and women the joy of living and the desire to foster and communicate life.

62. It is the duty of Christians therefore to remember that, although the practices of the Jewish Sabbath are gone, surpassed as they are by the "fulfilment" which Sunday brings, the underlying reasons for keeping "the

Lord's Day" holy — inscribed solemnly in the Ten Commandments — remain valid, though they need to be reinterpreted in the light of the theology and spirituality of Sunday: "Remember the Sabbath day to keep it holy, as the Lord your G_d commanded you. Six days you shall labour, and do all your work; but the seventh day is a Sabbath to the Lord your G_d. Then you shall do no work, you, or your son, or your daughter, or your servant, or your maid, or your ox, or your ass, or any of your beasts, or the foreigner within your gates, that your servant and maid may rest as well as you. You shall remember that you were a servant in the land of Egypt, and the Lord your G_d brought you out from there with a mighty hand and an outstretched arm. Therefore the Lord your G_d commanded that you keep the Sabbath day" (*Dt* 5:12-15). Here the Sabbath observance is closely linked with the liberation which G_d accomplished for his people.

63. Christ came to accomplish a new "exodus", to restore freedom to the oppressed. He performed many healings on the Sabbath (cf. *Mt* 12:9-14 and parallels), certainly not to violate the Lord's Day, but to reveal its full meaning: "The Sabbath was made for man, not man for the Sabbath" (*Mk* 2:27). Opposing the excessively

legalistic interpretation of some of his contemporaries, and developing the true meaning of the biblical Sabbath, Jesus, as "Lord of the Sabbath" (*Mk* 2:28), restores to the Sabbath observance its liberating character, carefully safeguarding the rights of G_d and the rights of man. This is why Christians, called as they are to proclaim the liberation won by the blood of Christ, felt that they had the authority to transfer the meaning of the Sabbath to the day of the Resurrection. The Passover of Christ has in fact liberated man from a slavery more radical than any weighing upon an oppressed people — the slavery of sin, which alienates man from G_d, and alienates man from himself and from others, constantly sowing within history the seeds of evil and violence.

The day of rest

64. For several centuries, Christians observed Sunday simply as a day of worship, without being able to give it the specific meaning of Sabbath rest. Only in the fourth century did the civil law of the Roman Empire recognize the weekly recurrence, determining that on "the day of the sun" the judges, the people of the cities

and the various trade corporations would not work. (107) Christians rejoiced to see thus removed the obstacles which until then had sometimes made observance of the Lord's Day heroic. They could now devote themselves to prayer in common without hindrance. (108)

It would therefore be wrong to see in this legislation of the rhythm of the week a mere historical circumstance with no special significance for the Church and which she could simply set aside. Even after the fall of the Empire, the Councils did not cease to insist upon the arrangements regarding Sunday rest. In countries where Christians are in the minority and where the festive days of the calendar do not coincide with Sunday, it is still Sunday which remains the Lord's Day, the day on which the faithful come together for the Eucharistic assembly. But this involves real sacrifices. For Christians it is not normal that Sunday, the day of joyful celebration, should not also be a day of rest, and it is difficult for them to keep Sunday holy if they do not have enough free time.

65. By contrast, the link between the Lord's Day and the

day of rest in civil society has a meaning and importance which go beyond the distinctly Christian point of view. The alternation between work and rest, built into human nature, is willed by G_d himself, as appears in the creation story in the Book of Genesis (cf. 2:2-3; *Ex* 20:8-11): rest is something "sacred", because it is man's way of withdrawing from the sometimes excessively demanding cycle of earthly tasks in order to renew his awareness that everything is the work of G_d. There is a risk that the prodigious power over creation which G_d gives to man can lead him to forget that G_d is the Creator upon whom everything depends. It is all the more urgent to recognize this dependence in our own time, when science and technology have so incredibly increased the power which man exercises through his work.

66. Finally, it should not be forgotten that even in our own day work is very oppressive for many people, either because of miserable working conditions and long hours — especially in the poorer regions of the world — or because of the persistence in economically more developed societies of too many cases of injustice and exploitation of man by man. When, through the centuries, she has made laws concerning Sunday rest,

(109) the Church has had in mind above all the work of servants and workers, certainly not because this work was any less worthy when compared to the spiritual requirements of Sunday observance, but rather because it needed greater regulation to lighten its burden and thus enable everyone to keep the Lord's Day holy. In this matter, my predecessor Pope Leo XIII in his Encyclical *Rerum Novarum* spoke of Sunday rest as a worker's right which the State must guarantee. (110)

In our own historical context there remains the obligation to ensure that everyone can enjoy the freedom, rest and relaxation which human dignity requires, together with the associated religious, family, cultural and interpersonal needs which are difficult to meet if there is no guarantee of at least one day of the week on which people can *both* rest and celebrate. Naturally, this right of workers to rest presupposes their right to work and, as we reflect on the question of the Christian understanding of Sunday, we cannot but recall with a deep sense of solidarity the hardship of countless men and women who, because of the lack of jobs, are forced to remain inactive on workdays as well.

67. Through Sunday rest, daily concerns and tasks can find their proper perspective: the material things about which we worry give way to spiritual values; in a moment of encounter and less pressured exchange, we see the true face of the people with whom we live. Even the beauties of nature — too often marred by the desire to exploit, which turns against man himself — can be rediscovered and enjoyed to the full. As the day on which man is at peace with G_d, with himself and with others, Sunday becomes a moment when people can look anew upon the wonders of nature, allowing themselves to be caught up in that marvellous and mysterious harmony which, in the words of Saint Ambrose, weds the many elements of the cosmos in a "bond of communion and peace" by "an inviolable law of concord and love". (111) Men and women then come to a deeper sense, as the Apostle says, that "everything created by G_d is good and nothing is to be rejected if it is received with thanksgiving, for then it is consecrated by the word of G_d and prayer" (*1 Tim* 4:4-5). If after six days of work — reduced in fact to five for many people — people look for time to relax and to pay more attention to other aspects of their lives, this corresponds to an authentic need which is in full harmony with the vision of the Gospel message. Believers are therefore called to satisfy this need in a way consistent with the

manifestation of their personal and community faith, as expressed in the celebration and sanctification of the Lord's Day.

Therefore, also in the particular circumstances of our own time, Christians will naturally strive to ensure that civil legislation respects their duty to keep Sunday holy. In any case, they are obliged in conscience to arrange their Sunday rest in a way which allows them to take part in the Eucharist, refraining from work and activities which are incompatible with the sanctification of the Lord's Day, with its characteristic joy and necessary rest for spirit and body. (112)

68. In order that rest may not degenerate into emptiness or boredom, it must offer spiritual enrichment, greater freedom, opportunities for contemplation and fraternal communion. Therefore, among the forms of culture and entertainment which society offers, the faithful should choose those which are most in keeping with a life lived in obedience to the precepts of the Gospel. Sunday rest then becomes "prophetic", affirming not only the absolute primacy of G_d, but also the primacy and dignity of the person with respect to the demands of

social and economic life, and anticipating in a certain sense the "new heavens" and the "new earth", in which liberation from slavery to needs will be final and complete. In short, the Lord's Day thus becomes in the truest sense *the day of man* as well.

A day of solidarity

69. Sunday should also give the faithful an opportunity to devote themselves to works of mercy, charity and apostolate. To experience the joy of the Risen Lord deep within is to share fully the love which pulses in his heart: there is no joy without love! Jesus himself explains this, linking the "new commandment" with the gift of joy: "If you keep my commandments, you will remain in my love, just as I have kept the Father's commandments and remain in his love. I have told you this that my own joy may be in you and your joy may be complete. This is my commandment: that you love one another as I have loved you" (*Jn* 15:10-12).

The Sunday Eucharist, therefore, not only does not absolve the faithful from the duties of charity, but on the contrary commits them even more "to all the works of charity, of mercy, of apostolic outreach, by means of which it is seen that the faithful of Christ are not of this world and yet are the light of the world, giving glory to the Father in the presence of men". (113)

70. Ever since Apostolic times, the Sunday gathering has in fact been for Christians a moment of fraternal sharing with the very poor. "On the first day of the week, each of you is to put aside and save whatever extra you earn" (*1 Cor* 16:2), says Saint Paul referring to the collection organized for the poor Churches of Judaea. In the Sunday Eucharist, the believing heart opens wide to embrace all aspects of the Church. But the full range of the apostolic summons needs to be accepted: far from trying to create a narrow "gift" mentality, Paul calls rather for a demanding *culture of sharing*, to be lived not only among the members of the community itself but also in society as a whole. (114) More than ever, we need to listen once again to the stern warning which Paul addresses to the community at Corinth, guilty of having humiliated the poor in the fraternal *agape* which accompanied "the Lord's Supper": "When you meet together, it is not the Lord's Supper that you eat. For in eating, each one goes ahead

with his own meal, and one is hungry and another is drunk. What! Do you not have houses to eat and drink in? Or do you despise the Church of G_d and humiliate those who have nothing?" (*1 Cor* 11:20-22). James is equally forceful in what he writes: "If a man with gold rings and in fine clothing comes into your assembly and a poor man in shabby clothing also comes in, and you pay attention to the one who wears the fine clothing and say, 'Take a seat here, please', while you say to the poor man, 'Stand there', or, 'Sit at my feet', have you not made distinctions among yourselves, and become judges with evil thoughts?" (2:2-4).

71. The teachings of the Apostles struck a sympathetic chord from the earliest centuries, and evoked strong echoes in the preaching of the Fathers of the Church. Saint Ambrose addressed words of fire to the rich who presumed to fulfil their religious obligations by attending church without sharing their goods with the poor, and who perhaps even exploited them: "You who are rich, do you hear what the Lord G_d says? Yet you come into church not to give to the poor but to take instead". (115) Saint John Chrysostom is no less demanding: "Do you wish to honour the body of Christ? Do not ignore him when he is naked. Do not

pay him homage in the temple clad in silk only then to neglect him outside where he suffers cold and nakedness. He who said: 'This is my body' is the same One who said: 'You saw me hungry and you gave me no food', and 'Whatever you did to the least of my brothers you did also to me' ... What good is it if the Eucharistic table is overloaded with golden chalices, when he is dying of hunger? Start by satisfying his hunger, and then with what is left you may adorn the altar as well". (116)

These words effectively remind the Christian community of the duty to make the Eucharist the place where fraternity becomes practical solidarity, where the last are the first in the minds and attentions of the brethren, where Christ himself — through the generous gifts from the rich to the very poor — may somehow prolong in time the miracle of the multiplication of the loaves. (117)

72. The Eucharist is an event and programme of true brotherhood. From the Sunday Mass there flows a tide of charity destined to spread into the whole life of the faithful, beginning by inspiring the very way in which

they live the rest of Sunday. If Sunday is a day of joy, Christians should declare by their actual behaviour that we cannot be happy "on our own". They look around to find people who may need their help. It may be that in their neighbourhood or among those they know there are sick people, elderly people, children or immigrants who precisely on Sundays feel more keenly their isolation, needs and suffering. It is true that commitment to these people cannot be restricted to occasional Sunday gestures. But presuming a wider sense of commitment, why not make the Lord's Day a more intense time of sharing, encouraging all the inventiveness of which Christian charity is capable? Inviting to a meal people who are alone, visiting the sick, providing food for needy families, spending a few hours in voluntary work and acts of solidarity: these would certainly be ways of bringing into people's lives the love of Christ received at the Eucharistic table.

73. Lived in this way, not only the Sunday Eucharist but the whole of Sunday becomes a great school of charity, justice and peace. The presence of the Risen Lord in the midst of his people becomes an undertaking of solidarity, a compelling force for inner renewal, an inspiration to change the structures of sin in which

individuals, communities and at times entire peoples are entangled. Far from being an escape, the Christian Sunday is a "prophecy" inscribed on time itself, a prophecy obliging the faithful to follow in the footsteps of the One who came "to preach good news to the poor, to proclaim release to captives and new sight to the blind, to set at liberty those who are oppressed, and to proclaim the acceptable year of the Lord" (*Lk* 4:18-19). In the Sunday commemoration of Easter, believers learn from Christ, and remembering his promise: "I leave you peace, my peace I give you" (*Jn* 14:27), they become in their turn *builders of peace*.

DIES DIERUM

CHAPTER V

Sunday: the Primordial Feast, Revealing the Meaning of Time

Christ the Alpha and Omega of time

74. "In Christianity time has a fundamental importance. Within the dimension of time the world was created; within it the history of salvation unfolds, finding its culmination in the 'fullness of time' of the Incarnation, and its goal in the glorious return of the Son of G_d at the end of time. In Jesus Christ, the Word made flesh, time becomes a dimension of G_d, who is himself eternal". (118)

In the light of the New Testament, the years of Christ's earthly life truly constitute the *centre of time*; this centre reaches its apex in the Resurrection. It is true that Jesus is G_d made man from the very moment of his conception in the womb of the Blessed Virgin, but only in the Resurrection is his humanity wholly transfigured and glorified, thus revealing the fullness of his divine identity and glory. In his speech in the synagogue at Antioch in Pisidia (cf. *Acts* 13:33), Paul applies the words of Psalm 2 to the Resurrection of Christ: "You are my Son, this day I have begotten you" (v. 7). It is precisely for this reason that, in celebrating the Easter Vigil, the Church acclaims the Risen Christ as "the Beginning and End, the Alpha and Omega". These are the words spoken by the celebrant as he prepares the Paschal candle, which bears the number of the current year. These words clearly attest that "Christ is the Lord of time; he is its beginning and its end; every year, every day and every moment are embraced by his Incarnation and Resurrection, and thus become part of the 'fullness of time'". (119)

75. Since Sunday is the weekly Easter, recalling and making present the day upon which Christ rose from the dead, it is also the day which reveals the meaning of time. It has nothing in common with the cosmic cycles according to which natural religion and human culture

tend to impose a structure on time, succumbing perhaps to the myth of eternal return. The Christian Sunday is wholly other! Springing from the Resurrection, it cuts through human time, the months, the years, the centuries, like a directional arrow which points them towards their target: Christ's Second Coming. Sunday foreshadows the last day, the day of the *Parousia*, which in a way is already anticipated by Christ's glory in the event of the Resurrection.

In fact, everything that will happen until the end of the world will be no more than an extension and unfolding of what happened on the day when the battered body of the Crucified Lord was raised by the power of the Spirit and became in turn the wellspring of the Spirit for all humanity. Christians know that there is no need to wait for another time of salvation, since, however long the world may last, they are already living in *the last times*. Not only the Church, but the cosmos itself and history are ceaselessly ruled and governed by the glorified Christ. It is this life-force which propels creation, "groaning in birth-pangs until now" (*Rom* 8:22), towards the goal of its full redemption. Mankind can have only a faint intuition of this process, but Christians have the key and the certainty. Keeping Sunday holy is the important witness which they are called to bear, so that every stage of human history will be upheld by hope.

Sunday in the Liturgical Year

76. With its weekly recurrence, the Lord's Day is rooted in the most ancient tradition of the Church and is vitally important for the Christian. But there was another rhythm which soon established itself: *the annual liturgical cycle.* Human psychology in fact desires the celebration of anniversaries, associating the return of dates and seasons with the remembrance of past events. When these events are decisive in the life of a people, their celebration generally creates a festive atmosphere which breaks the monotony of daily routine.

Now, by G_d's design, the great saving events upon which the Church's life is founded were closely linked to the annual Jewish feasts of Passover and Pentecost, and were prophetically foreshadowed in them. Since the second century, the annual celebration of Easter by Christians — having been added to the weekly Easter celebration — allowed a more ample meditation on the mystery of Christ crucified and risen. Preceded by a preparatory fast, celebrated in the course of a long vigil, extended into the fifty days leading to Pentecost, the feast of Easter — "solemnity of solemnities" — became the day *par excellence* for the initiation of catechumens. Through baptism they die to sin and rise to a new life because Jesus "was put to death for our sins and raised for our justification" (*Rom* 4:25; cf. 6:3-11). Intimately connected to the Paschal Mystery, the Solemnity of Pentecost takes on special importance, celebrating as it does the coming of the Holy Spirit upon the Apostles gathered with Mary and inaugurating the mission to all peoples. (120)

77. A similar commemorative logic guided the arrangement of the entire Liturgical Year. As the Second Vatican Council recalls, the Church wished to extend throughout the year "the entire mystery of Christ, from the Incarnation and Nativity to the Ascension, to the day of Pentecost and to the waiting in blessed hope for the return of the Lord. Remembering

in this way the mysteries of redemption, the Church opens to the faithful the treasury of the Lord's power and merits, making them present in some sense to all times, so that the faithful may approach them and be filled by them with the grace of salvation". (121)

After Easter and Pentecost, the most solemn celebration is undoubtedly the Nativity of the Lord, when Christians ponder the mystery of the Incarnation and contemplate the Word of G_d who deigns to assume our humanity in order to give us a share in his divinity.

78. Likewise, "in celebrating this annual cycle of the mysteries of Christ, the holy Church venerates with special love the Blessed Virgin Mary, Mother of G_d, united forever with the saving work of her Son". (122) In a similar way, by inserting into the annual cycle the commemoration of the martyrs and other saints on the occasion of their anniversaries, "the Church proclaims the Easter mystery of the saints who suffered with Christ and with him are now glorified". (123) When celebrated in the true spirit of the liturgy, the commemoration of the saints does not obscure the centrality of Christ, but on the contrary extols it,

demonstrating as it does the power of the redemption wrought by him. As Saint Paulinus of Nola sings, "all things pass, but the glory of the saints endures in Christ, who renews all things, while he himself remains unchanged". (124) The intrinsic relationship between the glory of the saints and that of Christ is built into the very arrangement of the Liturgical Year, and is expressed most eloquently in the fundamental and sovereign character of Sunday as the Lord's Day. Following the seasons of the Liturgical Year in the Sunday observance which structures it from beginning to end, the ecclesial and spiritual commitment of Christians comes to be profoundly anchored in Christ, in whom believers find their reason for living and from whom they draw sustenance and inspiration.

79. Sunday emerges therefore as the natural model for understanding and celebrating these feast-days of the Liturgical Year, which are of such value for the Christian life that the Church has chosen to emphasize their importance by making it obligatory for the faithful to attend Mass and to observe a time of rest, even though these feast-days may fall on variable days of the week. (125) Their number has been changed from time to time, taking into account social and economic

conditions, as also how firmly they are established in tradition, and how well they are supported by civil legislation. (126)

The present canonical and liturgical provisions allow each Episcopal Conference, because of particular circumstances in one country or another, to reduce the list of Holy Days of obligation. Any decision in this regard needs to receive the special approval of the Apostolic See, (127) and in such cases the celebration of a mystery of the Lord, such as the Epiphany, the Ascension or the Solemnity of the Body and Blood of Christ, must be transferred to Sunday, in accordance with liturgical norms, so that the faithful are not denied the chance to meditate upon the mystery. (128) Pastors should also take care to encourage the faithful to attend Mass on other important feast-days celebrated during the week. (129)

80. There is a need for special pastoral attention to the many situations where there is a risk that the popular and cultural traditions of a region may intrude upon the celebration of Sundays and other liturgical feast-days, mingling the spirit of genuine Christian faith with

elements which are foreign to it and may distort it. In such cases, catechesis and well-chosen pastoral initiatives need to clarify these situations, eliminating all that is incompatible with the Gospel of Christ. At the same time, it should not be forgotten that these traditions — and, by analogy, some recent cultural initiatives in civil society — often embody values which are not difficult to integrate with the demands of faith. It rests with the discernment of Pastors to preserve the genuine values found in the culture of a particular social context and especially in popular piety, so that liturgical celebration — above all on Sundays and holy days — does not suffer but rather may actually benefit. (130)

CONCLUSION

81. The spiritual and pastoral riches of Sunday, as it has been handed on to us by tradition, are truly great. When its significance and implications are understood in their entirety, Sunday in a way becomes a synthesis of the Christian life and a condition for living it well. It is clear therefore why the observance of the Lord's Day is so close to the Church's heart, and why in the Church's discipline it remains a real obligation. Yet more than as a precept, the observance should be seen as a need rising from the depths of Christian life. It is crucially important that all the faithful should be convinced that they cannot live their faith or share fully in the life of the Christian community unless they take part regularly in the Sunday Eucharistic assembly. The Eucharist is the full realization of the worship which humanity owes to G_d, and it cannot be compared to any other religious experience. A particularly efficacious expression of this is the Sunday gathering of the entire community, obedient to the voice of the Risen Lord who calls the faithful together to give them the light of his word and the nourishment of his Body as the perennial sacramental wellspring of redemption. The grace flowing from this wellspring renews mankind, life and history.

82. It is with this strong conviction of faith, and with awareness of the heritage of human values which the observance of Sunday entails, that Christians today must face the enticements of a culture which has accepted the benefits of rest and free time, but which often uses them frivolously and is at times attracted by morally questionable forms of entertainment. Certainly, Christians are no different from other people in enjoying the weekly day of rest; but at the same time they are keenly aware of the uniqueness and originality of Sunday, the day on which they are called to celebrate their salvation and the salvation of all humanity. Sunday is the day of joy and the day of rest precisely because it is "the Lord's Day", the day of the Risen Lord.

83. Understood and lived in this fashion, Sunday in a way becomes the soul of the other days, and in this sense we can recall the insight of Origen that the perfect Christian "is always in the Lord's Day, and is always celebrating Sunday". (131) Sunday is a true school, an enduring programme of Church pedagogy — an irreplaceable pedagogy, especially with social conditions now marked more and more by a fragmentation and cultural pluralism which constantly test the faithfulness of individual Christians to the

practical demands of their faith. In many parts of the world, we see a "diaspora" Christianity, which is put to the test because the scattered disciples of Christ can no longer easily maintain contact with one another, and lack the support of the structures and traditions proper to Christian culture. In a situation of such difficulty, the opportunity to come together on Sundays with fellow believers, exchanging gifts of brother- hood, is an indispensable help.

84. Sustaining Christian life as it does, Sunday has the additional value of being a testimony and a proclamation. As a day of prayer, communion and joy, Sunday resounds throughout society, emanating vital energies and reasons for hope. Sunday is the proclamation that time, in which he who is the Risen Lord of history makes his home, is not the grave of our illusions but the cradle of an ever new future, an opportunity given to us to turn the fleeting moments of this life into seeds of eternity. Sunday is an invitation to look ahead; it is the day on which the Christian community cries out to Christ, "*Marana tha*: Come, O Lord!" (*1 Cor* 16:22). With this cry of hope and expectation, the Church is the companion and support of human hope. From Sunday to Sunday, enlightened by

Christ, she goes forward towards the unending Sunday of the heavenly Jerusalem, which "has no need of the sun or moon to shine upon it, for the glory of G_d is its light and its lamp is the Lamb" (*Rev* 21:23).

85. As she strains towards her goal, the Church is sustained and enlivened by the Spirit. It is he who awakens memory and makes present for every generation of believers the event of the Resurrection. He is the inward gift uniting us to the Risen Lord and to our brothers and sisters in the intimacy of a single body, reviving our faith, filling our hearts with charity and renewing our hope. The Spirit is unfailingly present to every one of the Church's days, appearing unpredictably and lavishly with the wealth of his gifts. But it is in the Sunday gathering for the weekly celebration of Easter that the Church listens to the Spirit in a special way and reaches out with him to Christ in the ardent desire that he return in glory: "The Spirit and the Bride say, 'Come!'" (*Rev* 22:17). Precisely in consideration of the role of the Spirit, I have wished that this exhortation aimed at rediscovering the meaning of Sunday should appear in this year which, in the immediate preparation for the Jubilee, is dedicated to the Holy Spirit.

86. I entrust this Apostolic Letter to the intercession of the Blessed Virgin, that it may be received and put into practice by the Christian community. Without in any way detracting from the centrality of Christ and his Spirit, Mary is always present in the Church's Sunday. It is the mystery of Christ itself which demands this: indeed, how could she who is *Mater Domini* and *Mater Ecclesiae* fail to be uniquely present on the day which is both *dies Domini* and *dies Ecclesiae*?

As they listen to the word proclaimed in the Sunday assembly, the faithful look to the Virgin Mary, learning from her to keep it and ponder it in their hearts (cf. *Lk* 2:19). With Mary, they learn to stand at the foot of the Cross, offering to the Father the sacrifice of Christ and joining to it the offering of their own lives. With Mary, they experience the joy of the Resurrection, making their own the words of the Magnificat which extol the inexhaustible gift of divine mercy in the inexorable flow of time: "His mercy is from age to age upon those who fear him" (*Lk* 1:50). From Sunday to Sunday, the pilgrim people follow in the footsteps of Mary, and her maternal intercession gives special power and fervour to the prayer which rises from the Church to the Most Holy Trinity.

87. Dear Brothers and Sisters, the imminence of the Jubilee invites us to a deeper spiritual and pastoral commitment. Indeed, this is its true purpose. In the Jubilee year, much will be done to give it the particular stamp demanded by the ending of the Second Millennium and the beginning of the Third since the Incarnation of the Word of G_d. But this year and this special time will pass, as we look to other jubilees and other solemn events. As the weekly "solemnity", however, Sunday will continue to shape the time of the Church's pilgrimage, until that Sunday which will know no evening.

Therefore, dear Brother Bishops and Priests, I urge you to work tirelessly with the faithful to ensure that the value of this sacred day is understood and lived ever more deeply. This will bear rich fruit in Christian communities, and will not fail to have a positive influence on civil society as a whole.

In coming to know the Church, which every Sunday joyfully celebrates the mystery from which she draws her life, may the men and women of the Third Millennium come to know the Risen Christ. And constantly renewed by the weekly commemoration of Easter, may Christ's disciples be ever more credible in proclaiming the Gospel of salvation and ever more effective in building the civilization of love.

My blessing to you all!

From the Vatican, on 31 May, the Solemnity of Pentecost, in the year 1998, the twentieth of my Pontificate.

REFERENCE

This Apostolic letter can be viewed online at:
http://www.vatican.va/holy_father/john_paul_ii/apost_letters/documents/hf_jp-ii_apl_05071998_dies-domini_en.html

(1) Cf. *Rev* 1:10: "*Kyriake heméra*"; cf. also the *Didaché* 14, 1, Saint Ignatius of Antioch, *To the Magnesians* 9, 1-2; *SC* 10, 88-89.

(2) Pseudo-Eusebius of Alexandria, *Sermon* 16: *PG* 86, 416.

(3) *In Die Dominica Paschae II*, 52: *CCL* 78, 550.

(4) Second Vatican Ecumenical Council, Constitution on the Sacred Liturgy *Sacrosanctum Concilium*, 106.

(5) *Ibid*.

(6) Cf. Motu Proprio *Mysterii Paschalis* (14 February 1969): *AAS* 61 (1969), 222-226.

(7) Cf. Pastoral Note of the Italian Episcopal Conference "*Il giorno del Signore*" (15 July 1984), 5: *Enchiridion CEI* 3, 1398.

(8) Constitution on the Sacred Liturgy *Sacrosanctum Concilium*, 106.

(9) Homily for the Solemn Inauguration of the Pontificate (22 October 1978), 5: *AAS* 70 (1978), 947.

(10) No. 25: *AAS* 73 (1981), 639.

(11) Pastoral Constitution on the Church in the Modern World *Gaudium et Spes*, 34.

(12) For our Jewish brothers and sisters, a "nuptial" spirituality characterizes the Sabbath, as appears, for example, in texts of *Genesis Rabbah* such as X, 9 and

XI, 8 (cf. J. Neusner, *Genesis Rabbah*, vol. I, Atlanta 1985, p. 107 and p. 117). The song *Leka Dôdi* is also nuptial in tone: "Your G_d will delight in you, as the Bridegroom delights in the Bride ... In the midst of the faithful of your beloved people, come O Bride, O *Shabbat* Queen" (cf. *Preghiera serale del sabato*, issued by A. Toaff, Rome, 1968-69, p. 3).

(13) Cf. A. J. Heschel, *The Sabbath: Its Meaning for Modern Man* (22nd ed., 1995), pp. 3-24.

(14) "*Verum autem sabbatum ipsum redemptorem nostrum Iesum Christum Dominum habemus*": *Epist.* 13, 1: *CCL* 140A, 992.

(15) *Ep. ad Decentium* XXV, 4, 7: *PL* 20, 555.

(16) *Homiliae in Hexaemeron* II, 8: *SC* 26, 184.

(17) Cf. *In Io. Ev. Tractatus* XX, 20, 2: *CCL* 36, 203; *Epist.* 55, 2: *CSEL* 34, 170-171.

(18) The reference to the Resurrection is especially clear in Russian, which calls Sunday simply "Resurrection" (*Voskresenie*).

(19) *Epist.* 10, 96, 7.

(20) Cf. *ibid.* In reference to Pliny's letter, Tertullian also recalls the *coetus antelucani* in *Apologeticum* 2, 6: *CCL* 1, 88; *De Corona* 3, 3: *CCL* 2, 1043.

(21) *To the Magnesians* 9, 1-2: *SC* 10, 88-89.

(22) *Sermon 8 in the Octave of Easter* 4: *PL* 46, 841. This sense of Sunday as "the first day" is clear in the Latin liturgical calendar, where Monday is called *feria secunda*, Tuesday *feria tertia* and so on. In Portuguese, the days are named in the same way.

(23) Saint Gregory of Nyssa, *De Castigatione*: *PG* 46, 309. The Maronite Liturgy also stresses the link between the Sabbath and Sunday, beginning with the "mystery of Holy Saturday" (cf. M. Hayek, *Maronite*

[Eglise], Dictionnaire de spiritualité, X [1980], 632-644).]

(24) *Rite of Baptism of Children*, No. 9; cf. *Rite of Christian Initiation of Adults*, No. 59.

(25) Cf. *Roman Missal*, Rite of Blessing and Sprinkling of Holy Water.

(26) Cf. Saint Basil, *On the Holy Spirit*, 27, 66: *SC* 17, 484-485. Cf. also *Letter of Barnabas* 15, 8-9: *SC* 172, 186-189; Saint Justin, *Dialogue with Trypho* 24; 138: *PG* 6, 528, 793; Origen, *Commentary on the Psalms*, Psalm 118(119), 1: *PG* 12, 1588.

(27) "*Domine, praestitisti nobis pacem quietis, pacem sabbati, pacem sine vespera*": *Confess.*, 13, 50: *CCL* 27, 272.

(28) Cf. Saint Augustine, *Epist.* 55, 17: *CSEL* 34, 188: "*Ita ergo erit octavus, qui primus, ut prima vita sed aeterna reddatur*".

(29) Thus in English "Sunday" and in German "*Sonntag*".

(30) *Apologia I*, 67: *PG* 6, 430.

(31) Cf. Saint Maximus of Turin, *Sermo* 44, 1: *CCL* 23, 178; *Sermo* 53, 2: *CCL* 23, 219; Eusebius of Caesarea, *Comm. in Ps.* 91: *PG* 23, 1169-1173.

(32) See, for example, the Hymn of the Office of Readings: "*Dies aetasque ceteris octava splendet sanctior in te quam, Iesu, consecras primitiae surgentium* (Week I); and also: "*Salve dies, dierum gloria, dies felix Christi victoria, dies digna iugi laetitia dies prima. Lux divina caecis irradiat, in qua Christus infernum spoliat, mortem vincit et reconciliat summis ima*" (Week II). Similar expressions are found in hymns included in the Liturgy of the Hours in various modern languages.

(33) Cf. Clement of Alexandria, *Stromata*, VI, 138, 1-2: *PG* 9, 364.

(34) Cf. John Paul II, Encyclical Letter *Dominum et Vivificantem* (18 May 1986), 22-26: *AAS* 78 (1986), 829-837.

(35) Cf. Saint Athanasius of Alexandria, *Sunday Letters* 1, 10: *PG* 26, 1366.

(36) Cf. Bardesanes, *Dialogue on Destiny*, 46: *PS* 2, 606-607.

(37) Constitution on the Sacred Liturgy *Sacrosanctum Concilium*, Appendix: Declaration on the Reform of the Calendar.

(38) Cf. Second Vatican Ecumenical Council, Dogmatic Constitution on the Church *Lumen Gentium*, 9.

(39) Cf. John Paul II, Letter *Dominicae Cenae* (24 February 1980), 4: *AAS* 72 (1980), 120; Encyclical Letter *Dominum et Vivificantem* (18 May 1986), 62-64: *AAS* 78 (1986), 889-894.

(40) Cf. John Paul II, Apostolic Letter *Vicesimus Quintus Annus* (4 December 1988), 9: *AAS* 81 (1989), 905-906.

(41) No. 2177.

(42) Cf. John Paul II, Apostolic Letter *Vicesimus Quintus Annus* (4 December 1988), 9: *AAS* 81 (1989), 905-906.

(43) Second Vatican Ecumenical Council, Constitution on the Sacred Liturgy *Sacrosanctum Concilium*, 41; cf. Decree on the Pastoral Office of Bishops in the Church *Christus Dominus*, 15.

(44) These are the words of the Embolism, formulated in this or similar ways in some of the Eucharistic Prayers of the different languages. They stress powerfully the "Paschal" character of Sunday.

(45) Cf. Congregation for the Doctrine of the Faith, Letter to the Bishops of the Catholic Church on Certain

Aspects of the Church as Communion *Communionis Notio* (28 May 1992), 11-14: *AAS* 85 (1993), 844-847.

(46) *Speech to the Third Group of the Bishops of the United States of America* (17 March 1998), 4: *L'Osservatore Romano*, 18 March 1998, 4.

(47) Constitution on the Sacred Liturgy *Sacrosanctum Concilium*, 42.

(48) Sacred Congregation of Rites, Instruction on the Worship of the Eucharistic Mystery *Eucharisticum Mysterium* (25 May 1967), 26: *AAS* 59 (1967), 555.

(49) Cf. Saint Cyprian, *De Orat. Dom.* 23: *PL* 4, 553; *De Cath. Eccl. Unitate*, 7: *CSEL* 31, 215; Second Vatican Ecumenical Council, Dogmatic Constitution on the Church *Lumen Gentium*, 4; Constitution on the Sacred Liturgy *Sacrosanctum Concilium*, 26.

(50) Cf. John Paul II, Apostolic Exhortation *Familiaris Consortio* (22 November 1981), 57; 61: *AAS* 74 (1982),

151; 154.

(51) Cf. Sacred Congregation for Divine Worship, *Directory for Masses with Children* (1 November 1973): *AAS* 66 (1974), 30-46.

(52) Cf. Sacred Congregation of Rites, Instruction on the Worship of the Eucharistic Mystery *Eucharisticum Mysterium* (25 May 1967), 26: *AAS* 59 (1967), 555-556; Sacred Congregation for Bishops, Directory for the Pastoral Ministry of Bishops *Ecclesiae Imago* (22 February 1973), 86c: *Enchiridion Vaticanum* 4, 2071.

(53) Cf. John Paul II, Post-Synodal Apostolic Exhortation *Christifideles Laici* (30 December 1988), 30: *AAS* 81 (1989), 446-447.

(54) Cf. Sacred Congregation for Divine Worship, Instruction *Masses for Particular Groups* (15 May 1969), 10: *AAS* 61 (1969), 810.

(55) Cf. Second Vatican Ecumenical Council, Dogmatic

Constitution on the Church *Lumen Gentium*, 48-51.

(56) "*Haec est vita nostra, ut desiderando exerceamur*": Saint Augustine, *In Prima Ioan. Tract.* 4, 6: *SC* 75, 232.

(57) *Roman Missal*, Embolism after the Lord's Prayer.

(58) Second Vatican Ecumenical Council, Pastoral Constitution on the Church in the Modern World *Gaudium et Spes*, 1.

(59) Second Vatican Ecumenical Council, Dogmatic Constitution on the Church *Lumen Gentium*, 1; cf. John Paul II, Encyclical Letter *Dominum et Vivificantem* (18 May 1986), 61-64: *AAS* 78 (1986), 888-894.

(60) Second Vatican Ecumenical Council, Constitution on the Sacred Liturgy *Sacrosanctum Concilium*, 7; cf. 33.

(61) *Ibid.*, 56; cf. *Ordo Lectionum Missae,*

Praenotanda, No. 10.

(62) Constitution on the Sacred Liturgy *Sacrosanctum Concilium*, 51.

(63) Cf. *ibid.*, 52; *Code of Canon Law*, Canon 767, 2; *Code of Canons of the Eastern Churches*, Canon 614.

(64) Apostolic Constitution *Missale Romanum* (3 April 1969): *AAS* 61 (1969), 220.

(65) The Council's Constitution *Sacrosanctum Concilium* speaks of "*suavis et vivus Sacrae Scripturae affectus*" (No. 24).

(66) John Paul II, Letter *Dominicae Cenae* (24 February 1980), 10: *AAS* 72 (1980), 135.

(67) Cf. Second Vatican Ecumenical Council, Dogmatic Constitution on Divine Revelation *Dei Verbum*, 25.

(68) Cf. *Ordo Lectionum Missae, Praenotanda*, Chap. III.

(69) Cf. *Ordo Lectionum Missae, Praenotanda*, Chap. I, No. 6.

(70) Ecumenical Council of Trent, *Session XXII, Doctrine and Canons on the Most Holy Sacrifice of the Mass*, II: *DS* 1743; cf. *Catechism of the Catholic Church*, 1366.

(71) *Catechism of the Catholic Church*, 1368.

(72) Sacred Congregation of Rites, Instruction on the Worship of the Eucharistic Mystery *Eucharisticum Mysterium* (25 May 1967), 3b: *AAS* 59 (1967), 541; cf. Pius XII, Encyclical Letter *Mediator Dei* (20 November 1947), II: *AAS* 39 (1947), 564-566.

(73) Cf. *Catechism of the Catholic Church*, 1385; cf. also Congregation for the Doctrine of the Faith, *Letter to the Bishops of the Catholic Church concerning the*

Reception of Eucharistic Communion by Divorced and Remarried Faithful (14 September 1994): *AAS* 86 (1994), 974-979.

(74) Cf. Innocent I, *Epist.* 25, 1 to Decentius of Gubbio: *PL* 20, 553.

(75) II, 59, 2-3: ed. F. X. Funk, 1905, pp. 170-171.

(76) Cf. *Apologia I*, 67, 3-5: *PG* 6, 430.

(77) *Acta SS. Saturnini, Dativi et aliorum plurimorum Martyrum in Africa*, 7, 9, 10: *PL* 8, 707, 709-710.

(78) Cf. Canon 21, Mansi, *Conc.* II, 9.

(79) Cf. Canon 47, Mansi, *Conc.* VIII, 332.

(80) Cf. the contrary proposition, condemned by Innocent XI in 1679, concerning the moral obligation to

keep the feast-day holy: *DS* 2152.

(81) Canon 1248: "*Festis de praecepto diebus Missa audienda est*": Canon 1247, 1: "*Dies festi sub praecepto in universa Ecclesia sunt...omnes et singuli dies dominici*".

(82) *Code of Canon Law*, Canon 1247; the *Code of Canons of the Eastern Churches*, Canon 881, 1, prescribes that "the Christian faithful are bound by the obligation to participate on Sundays and feast days in the Divine Liturgy or, according to the prescriptions or legitimate customs of their own Church *sui iuris,* in the celebration of the divine praises".

(83) No. 2181: "Those who deliberately fail in this obligation commit a grave sin".

(84) Sacred Congregation for Bishops, Directory for the Pastoral Ministry of Bishops *Ecclesiae Imago* (22 February 1973), 86a: *Enchiridion Vaticanum* 4, 2069.

(85) Cf. *Code of Canon Law*, Canon 905, 2.

(86) Cf. Pius XII, Apostolic Constitution *Christus Dominus* (6 January 1953): *AAS* 45 (1953), 15-24; Motu Proprio *Sacram Communionem* (19 March 1957): *AAS* 49 (1957), 177-178. Congregation of the Holy Office, Instruction on the Discipline concerning the Eucharist Fast (6 January 1953): *AAS* 45 (1953), 47-51.

(87) Cf. *Code of Canon Law*, Canon 1248, 1; *Code of Canons of the Eastern Churches*, Canon 881, 2.

(88) Cf. *Missale Romanum, Normae Universales de Anno Liturgico et de Calendario*, 3.

(89) Cf. Sacred Congregation of Bishops, Directory for the Pastoral Ministry of Bishops *Ecclesiae Imago* (22 February 1973), 86: *Enchiridion Vaticanum* 4, 2069-2073.

(90) Cf. Second Vatican Ecumenical Council, Constitution on the Sacred Liturgy *Sacrosanctum*

Concilium, 14; 26; John Paul II, Apostolic Letter *Vicesimus Quintus Annus* (4 December 1988), 4; 6; 12: *AAS* 81 (1989), 900-901; 902; 909-910.

(91) Cf. Second Vatican Ecumenical Council, Dogmatic Constitution on the Church *Lumen Gentium*, 10.

(92) Cf. Interdicasterial Instruction on Certain Questions concerning the Collaboration of Lay Faithful in the Ministry of Priests *Ecclesiae de Mysterio* (15 August 1997), 6; 8: *AAS* 89 (1997), 869; 870-872.

(93) Second Vatican Ecumenical Council, Dogmatic Constitution on the Church *Lumen Gentium*, 10: "*in oblationem Eucharistiae concurrunt*".

(94) *Ibid.*, 11.

(95) Cf. *Code of Canon Law*, Canon 1248, 2.

(96) Cf. Sacred Congregation for Divine Worship,

Directory for Sunday Celebrations in the Absence of a Priest *Christi Ecclesia* (2 June 1988): *Enchiridion Vaticanum* 11, 442-468; Interdicasterial Instruction on Certain Questions concerning the Collaboration of Lay Faithful in the Ministry of Priests *Ecclesiae de Mysterio* (15 August 1997): *AAS* 89 (1997), 852-877.

(97) Cf. *Code of Canon Law*, Canon 1248, 2; Congregation for the Doctrine of the Faith, Letter *Sacerdotium Ministeriale* (6 August 1983), III: *AAS* 75 (1983), 1007.

(98) Cf. Pontifical Commission for Social Communications, Instruction *Communio et Progressio* (23 May 1971), 150-152; 157: *AAS* 63 (1971), 645-646; 647.

(99) This is the Deacon's proclamation in honour of the Lord's Day: cf. the Syriac text in the Missal of the Church of Antioch of the Maronites (edition in Syriac and Arabic), Jounieh (Lebanon) 1959, p. 38.

(100) V, 20, 11: ed. F. X. Funk, 1905, p. 298; cf. *Didache* 14, 1: ed. F. X. Funk, 1901, p. 32; Tertullian, *Apologeticum* 16, 11: *CCL* 1, 116. See in particular the *Epistle of Barnabas*, 15, 9: *SC* 172, 188-189: "This is why we celebrate as a joyous feast the eighth day on which Jesus was raised from the dead and, after having appeared, ascended into heaven".

(101) Tertullian for example tells us that on Sunday it was forbidden to kneel, since kneeling, which was then seen as an essentially penitential gesture, seemed unsuited to the day of joy. Cf. *De Corona* 3, 4: *CCL* 2, 1043.

(102) *Ep.* 55, 28: *CSEL* 342, 202.

(103) Cf. Saint Therese of the Child Jesus and the Holy Face, *Derniers entretiens*, 5-6 July 1897, in: *Oeuvres complètes*, Cerf - Desclée de Brouwer, Paris, 1992, pp. 1024-1025.

(104) Apostolic Exhortation, *Gaudete in Domino* (9

May 1975), II: *AAS* 67 (1975), 295.

(105) *Ibid.* VII, *l.c.*, 322.

(106) *Hex.* 6, 10, 76: *CSEL* 321, 261.

(107) Cf. The Edict of Constantine, 3 July 321: *Codex Theodosianus* II, tit. 8, 1, ed. T. Mommsen, 12, p. 87; *Codex Iustiniani*, 3, 12, 2, ed. P. Krueger, p. 248.

(108) Cf. Eusebius of Caesarea, *Life of Constantine*, 4, 18: *PG* 20, 1165.

(109) The most ancient text of this kind is can. 29 of the Council of Laodicea (second half of the fourth century): Mansi, II, 569-570. From the sixth to the ninth century, many Councils prohibited "*opera ruralia*". The legislation on prohibited activities, supported by civil laws, became increasingly detailed.

(110) Cf. Encyclical Letter *Rerum Novarum* (15 May

1891): *Acta Leonis XIII* 11 (1891), 127-128.

(111) *Hex.* 2, 1, 1: *CSEL* 321, 41.

(112) Cf. *Code of Canon Law*, Canon 1247; *Code of Canons of the Eastern Churches*, Canon 881, 1; 4.

(113) Second Vatican Ecumenical Council, Constitution on the Sacred Liturgy *Sacrosanctum Concilium*, 9.

(114) Cf. also Saint Justin, *Apologia I*, 67, 6: "Each of those who have an abundance and who wish to make an offering gives freely whatever he chooses, and what is collected is given to him who presides and he assists the orphans, the widows, the sick, the poor, the prisoners, the foreign visitors — in a word, he helps all those who are in need": *PG* 6, 430.

(115) *De Nabuthae*, 10, 45: "*Audis, dives, quid Dominus Deus dicat? Et tu ad ecclesiam venis, non ut aliquid largiaris pauperi, sed ut auferas*": CSEL 322, 492.

(116) *Homilies on the Gospel of Matthew*, 50, 3-4: *PG* 58, 508-509.

(117) Saint Paulinus of Nola, *Ep.* 13, 11-12 to Pammachius: *CSEL* 29, 92-93. The Roman Senator is praised because, by combining participation in the Eucharist with distribution of food to the poor, he in a sense reproduced the Gospel miracle.

(118) John Paul II, Apostolic Letter *Tertio Millennio Adveniente* (10 November 1994), 10: *AAS* 87 (1995), 11.

(119) *Ibid.*

(120) Cf. *Catechism of the Catholic Church*, 731-732.

(121) Constitution on the Sacred Liturgy *Sacrosanctum Concilium*, 102.

(122) *Ibid.*, 103.

(123) *Ibid.*, 104.

(124) *Carm.* XVI, 3-4: "*Omnia praetereunt, sanctorum gloria durat in Christo qui cuncta novat, dum permanet ipse*": *CSEL* 30, 67.

(125) Cf. *Code of Canon Law*, Canon 1247; *Code of Canons of the Eastern Churches*, Canon 881, 1; 4.

(126) By general law, the holy days of obligation in the Latin Church are the Feasts of the Nativity of the Lord, the Epiphany, the Ascension, the Body and Blood of Christ, Mary Mother of G_d, the Immaculate Conception, the Assumption, Saint Joseph, Saints Peter and Paul and All Saints: cf. *Code of Canon Law*, Canon 1246. The holy days of obligation in all the Eastern Churches are the Feasts of the Nativity of the Lord, the Epiphany, the Ascension, the Dormition of Mary Mother of G_d and Saints Peter and Paul: cf. *Code of Canons of the Eastern Churches*, Canon 880, 3.

(127) Cf. *Code of Canon Law*, Canon 1246, 2; for the Eastern Churches, cf. *Code of Canons of the Eastern Churches,* Canon 880, 3.

(128) Cf. Sacred Congregation of Rites, *Normae Universales de Anno Liturgico et de Calendario* (21 March 1969), 5, 7: *Enchiridion Vaticanum* 3, 895; 897.

(129) Cf. *Caeremoniale Episcoporum*, ed. typica 1995, No. 230.

(130) Cf. *ibid.*, No. 233.

(131) *Contra Celsum* VIII, 22: *SC* 150, 222-224.

m VIII, 22: *SC* 150, 222-224.

(131) *Contra Celsum* VIII, 22: *SC* 150, 222-224.

Liturgico et de Calendario (21 March 1969), 5, 7: *Enchiridion Vaticanum* 3, 895; 897.

(129) Cf. *Caeremoniale Episcoporum*, ed. typica 1995, No. 230.

(130) Cf. *ibid.*, No. 233.

(131) *Contra Celsum* VIII, 22: *SC* 150, 222-224.

Made in the USA
Monee, IL
14 February 2023